How to Pastor
and
Live to Tell about It

Lessons from Nehemiah

How to Pastor
and
Live to Tell about It

Lessons from Nehemiah

Roberta Sarver

Name: Roberta Sarver
Title: How to Pastor and Live to Tell about It: Lessons from Nehemiah/ By Roberta Sarver
Identifiers: LCCN: XXXXXXXXXX
ISBN: 978-1-955309-40-0
Subjects: 1. Church Leadership/Administration
2. Pastoral Resources/Clergy
3. Nehemiah/Biblical Studies

Scripture quotations from The Authorized (King James) Version. Rights in the Authorized Version in the United Kingdom are vested in the Crown.
Reproduced by permission of the Crown's patentee, Cambridge University Press.

"Celestial Piano Lessons" reproduced by permission of Abundance Books. Further reproduction, distribution or transmission is prohibited, except as otherwise permitted by law.

Cover Design & Production by Robert Scott / Clear Graphics (859) 907-7835

Alan Parry Cover art used with permission from (c) Bill Noller International Publishing, Castle Rock, CO 80108

Published by EA Books Publishing a division of
Living Parables of Central Florida, Inc. a 501c3
EABooksPublishing.com

DEDICATION

To the faithful ministers who feed and guard souls each week. You labor in the trenches, pray for us when we're down, and celebrate our victories. No one ever said your job would be easy. Thank you for not giving up on your flock.

To those who faithfully and lovingly mentored a young girl searching for God's truth during a cultural revolution many years ago. To the unsung heroes of the faith who loved my soul enough to tell me the truth, and who lived it daily. To the Bible college teachers and pastors who opened God's Word so skillfully.

To those who dared to walk against popular opinion, thus challenging my thinking. Though unnamed here, you have your reward in heaven. And to those still living who dare to take the road less traveled by, may your tribe increase.

TABLE OF CONTENTS

PREFACE

If you're reading this book, you probably skimmed the back cover and thought, *hmm, maybe this has the answer to my problem with* (fill in situation or someone's name).

Perhaps you're having relationship challenges with someone in your church and don't know how to proceed. Or maybe there are no issues right now, but you anticipate some in the future. If that describes your situation, this book is for you.

Insights into human nature—you'll find them here. Nehemiah, one of God's leaders in biblical times, handled things in unique ways. He rubbed elbows with those whose thinking differed from his own. Many of the issues he encountered parallel those that heads of organizations struggle with today.

After observing pastors for many years, I know what it's like to watch them cope with challenges. The constant strain can drain a shepherd's emotional energy.

In this book you will find stories of real people in our times who faced leadership issues like Nehemiah's, because human problems are the same, no matter the era. Most names have been changed to protect the pastors who shared their experiences.

You are invited to turn these pages and discover amazing insights and solutions based on the leadership model of the man Nehemiah. And hopefully, you will discover perspectives that open a door of freedom for you and those involved.

DISCLAIMER

A wise employer once said, "You can learn something from everyone, even if it's how *not* to do something." Therefore, I issue this disclaimer: *Use of various pastors' writings in this book does not constitute an endorsement of their views on everything.* I asked for their experiences; they kindly responded. Read their thoughts, glean what you can, and ask God for wisdom.

CHAPTER ONE

What's a Nice Guy Like You Doin' in a Place Like This?

Len transitioned from pastoring a country congregation to a cosmopolitan one. He found his ministry exciting, except for one unique challenge. The former pastor and his family still attended the church and held important positions. Though his predecessor may not have intended to interfere, Len's divergent personality and methods caused roadblocks when he tried to address problems. If he handled situations differently than the former pastor, dismayed church members approached "Old Brother B" expecting him to intervene. Len discovered that ministering in a beloved pastor's shadow could be daunting. The situation finally resolved after a few years when Old Brother B and his wife moved to another state.

This young minister's situation wasn't unique. Several centuries prior, another leader, servant to the king in the world's most powerful empire, also encountered stress-producing situations. He faced people who challenged his leadership and criticized his decisions. Despite impossible circumstances, this groundbreaking leader motivated discouraged workers, corrected unfavorable living conditions, and reformed faulty worship practices. He guided the Jewish people in recovering their national identity after they lived in exile for several decades.

Who Was He? Nehemiah, the Ancient Nonconformist

In this book we will explore Nehemiah's methods as they apply to pastoral leadership. Later chapters will describe strategies that Pastor Len and others like him could use to resolve prickly situations, following Nehemiah's model. We will even discuss this unique leader's hair-pulling incident in chapter twelve of this book. Several modern-day servant

1

leaders with pastoral experience have added their insights; you will find them spliced within these chapters.

Have *you* ever wondered how your denominational officials decided to appoint you to the position you hold in your church? Or perhaps how someone even considered you for the job? If *overwhelmed* is in your vocabulary, you're not alone.

In the fifth century before Christ, the Jewish exile Nehemiah lived in Persia and served as cupbearer to King Artaxerxes. His position was both prestigious and dangerous. Each time the king dined, his cupbearer tasted the monarch's food and drink to test for poison. Nehemiah became one of the king's closest companions, first to hear and report court gossip, a sort of ancient network reporter. Some even tried to convince men in his position to elicit favors from the king.[1]

That wasn't all that was required of the king's cupbearer. Some scholars tell us men in Nehemiah's position served as "a kind of prime minister and master of ceremonies, both in one…the royal favorite above all the rest of the palace."[2] Obviously, his job required wisdom and tact.

Bible scholars think Nehemiah was born into an influential family who'd been forced into exile when the Assyrians ransacked Jerusalem before he was born. His ancestors had to trek 800 miles to a foreign land and assimilate as slaves in a pagan culture. However, Nehemiah and others kept their allegiance to the God of the Israelites. His diplomacy and keen insight came from a dedicated walk with the God of heaven.

We don't know if this loyal Jewish man had a precedent to follow as the king's cupbearer. We do know serious mistakes in front of the king could get a person killed.

Though your position may not get you killed (or maybe it feels like it could), you ponder all the ramifications your actions could have. Will those around you suffer for what you do? How will leadership affect your family? Are you equal to the task?

In quiet moments, leaders sometimes wonder what the powers that be were thinking when they chose them to pastor the church, lead the Bible study, or spearhead the organization. They feel like deer in the headlights, knowing their leadership style may not mirror those who preceded them. And that could lead to conflicts.

Not all leaders appear to have what the world considers qualifications for leadership. Yet God uses them in unusual ways.

God Doesn't Call the Qualified—He Qualifies the Called

Charlotte Elliott of Brighton, England, was an invalid in 1834. Her brother organized a charity bazaar, with the proceeds going to provide higher education for daughters of clergymen. Those around Charlotte were busy preparing for the grand event, while she despaired at her apparent uselessness. Deciding to concentrate instead on her salvation in Christ, Charlotte wrote the poem "Just As I Am." Now one of the most widely used invitation hymns ever, Charlotte's simple poem has traveled around the world.[3]

In another instance, Haskell was a quiet, humble young man enrolled in ministry training in the mid-1900s. While there, he felt a call from God to minister to unchurched people in Mexico. The problem was, he seemed a most unlikely candidate for the rigors of missionary life. Childhood polio left him with a limp. His young wife had an eye disease that eventually would leave her blind.

No mission organization would take a risk on Haskell and his wife; her health was too delicate. And though he kept the calling before God in prayer, as their five children arrived, the risks multiplied. Instead, they pastored churches and waited twelve years for the God of heaven to open doors.

Eventually, Haskell and his wife did go to the mission field. This unique couple pioneered seven flourishing churches that still exist in the mountains of Mexico today. Now, more than thirty-five years later, men who became Christians in those indigenous churches serve as their pastors.

Another Improbable Example

Perhaps most inconceivable of all candidates for leadership was Dwight L. Moody. Most remember him as the beloved preacher, evangelist, and founder of schools as well as the famous Moody Church in Chicago. He wasn't always a stalwart candidate for headship, however.

Moody had a less-than-ideal start. His father died when Dwight was four, leaving the boy's mother with nine children to raise (a set of twins was born only a month after their father's death). Dwight attended school only through fifth grade.

At age seventeen, the boy grew bored with life on the farm and sought employment in the outside world. Several employers rejected him until finally he found work in his uncle's shoe store. Fortunately, this uncle required Dwight to attend Sunday school. His Sunday school teacher, Edward Kimball, said this:

> I can truly say, and in saying it I magnify the infinite grace of God as bestowed upon him, that I have seen few persons whose minds were spiritually darker than was his when he came into my Sunday school class; I think that the committee of the Mount Vernon Church seldom met an applicant for membership more unlikely ever to become a Christian of clear and decided views of Gospel truth, still less to fill any extended sphere of public usefulness.[4]

Clearly, young Dwight seemed unfit for any type of Christian service. Despite Moody's apparent lack of leadership abilities, he applied himself to soul winning. This young convert convinced a saloonkeeper to let him use an abandoned shanty where he began a Sunday school for working-class children.

A year later, 650 people attended his Sunday school, with sixty teachers from various churches serving as volunteers.

Moody once quipped, "If this world is going to be reached, I am convinced that it must be done by men and women of average talent."

God Uses Ordinary People to Confound Those Considered Wise

And then there was Ella Zuch, my spiritual mentor. Those who didn't know this tiny woman might assume she was unsuitable for any leadership role. In spite of her quiet, humble, and ordinary appearance, she served on a Bible college advisory board and helped prepare a Christian retreat center and camp for decades of useful service.

The first thing people noticed about Ella was her height—or lack of it. Standing less than five feet tall, she used her hands and back to help James, her preacher-husband and their friends, H. Robb and Geraldine French, to clear an overgrown, junglelike piece of property in the obscure village of Hobe Sound, Florida. Later this location would house an annual Christian camp meeting and the Bible college campus where I studied.

Ella was a surprise package. I once heard her say she wanted to make sure she was dead to pride, so she sewed a few dresses out of fabric she didn't like. Though not everyone would embrace that mindset, I discovered that behind her ordinary, plain appearance existed a delightful intellect and a treasure trove of wisdom. Her peaceful countenance radiated a close walk with the Lord.

My job was to drive this saintly lady forty-five minutes to a small church in Riviera Beach, Florida, each Sunday. During those trips Ella described teaching in a one-room school in the state of New York when she was young. She often applied deep principles from God's Word to everyday occurrences. Those solid spiritual insights spurred me, a new Christian, to learn all I could about applying God's Word to daily living.

The Nehemiah Principle

In ancient times, onlookers might have considered Nehemiah an unlikely candidate for motivating a ragtag group of exiles to accomplish a gargantuan task. He had to travel 800 miles to Jerusalem, sweat a lot, and work side by side with his fellow countrymen to rebuild shattered walls. In contrast to life in the palace surrounded by sumptuous wealth, he grew hot and tired. His workers became discouraged. The project demanded dealing with delicate and complicated situations. He had to solve disputes involving problematic people.

Pastor, Nehemiah may have felt just like *you* do at times. His success came as he looked to the One who called him to the task in the first place. So, if you're thinking, *Maybe God can use me despite my weaknesses,* you're in good company. You never can tell what the Lord will do with an obedient heart and willing hands.

Years ago, we held a vacation Bible school for children and needed a song to fit our theme. These words came to me, and I set them to music.

Little Things

God likes to use the little things to see His work is done.
He always gets the glory when we exalt His Son.
Just use the thing that's in your hand and let Him do the rest.
God likes to use the little things to show His way is best.

God likes to use the little things to see His work is done.
He used Elijah's cruse of oil to feed the widow's sons.
He used David's shepherd's sling along with five smooth stones
To kill a giant nine feet tall, the glory God's alone.

A tent peg in a woman's hand put Sisera to sleep.
Moses' rod up in the air drowned Pharaoh in the deep.
Five loaves and two small fish were giv'n from a small boy's lunch.
He gave it; Jesus multiplied, to feed that hungry bunch.

A little coin found in a fish paid Christ's disciples' tax.
A widow's mite was blessed by Him; she was never lax.
A little maid to Naaman's wife helped them to find a cure.
Can God in heaven use me then? O yes, you can be sure.
c. 2022 Roberta Sarver

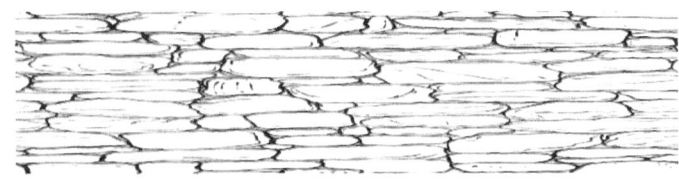

Dear Father in Heaven, You said in Your Word that You would equip us for the tasks given to us. I am asking for wisdom to handle all You allow to come across my pathway. In I Corinthians 1:26 and 27 You tell us, "For ye see your calling, brethren, how that not many wise men after the flesh, not many mighty, not many noble, are called: But God hath chosen the foolish things of the world to confound the wise; and God hath chosen the weak things of the world to confound the things which are mighty" (KJV).

That's where I fit in, Lord. I don't know how to handle all that comes with my calling. Please help me to be Christ-like in my actions and reactions when I come across those whose thinking is different than mine. Through the name of Jesus, amen.

CHAPTER TWO

But Lord, I Was Just Doing My Job!

Sometimes pastors and leaders find themselves in prickly situations (yes, I see those hands). There is no one-size-fits-all method for handling complicated human relationships—especially when it involves petitioning the king (or the board of elders) for a tremendous building project, along with the materials to complete it. Timing was and is crucial.

Prayer and timing are crucial in most tasks involving ministry. The narrative below continues Haskell's story from chapter one, in his own words. Just so you know, Haskell is his real name.

Living by Faith

God taught my wife and me to live by faith, to trust Him to supply all our needs while still in Bible college, preparing to be missionaries.

I worked at a bindery; part of my job was repairing books and magazines. While doing this, I saw I was binding advertisements for cigarettes and beer. God caused me to feel condemned and troubled for having a part in advertising these things.

I asked my boss if this had to be a part of my work, because I didn't believe it pleased the Lord. He said if I worked there, I would have to do it. So, I told him I would be quitting in two weeks. He said nothing; perhaps he thought I wasn't serious, since jobs were hard to find.

Two weeks passed. I thanked my boss for the job and told him I would not be returning to work. He acted very surprised and asked, "What are you going to do for a job?" I told him I didn't know, but I believed God would make a way for my family and me.

I went home and my wife met me at the door. "Why are you home so soon?" she asked. I told her about quitting my job.

I went into our bedroom and knelt to pray, knowing God had initiated what I did. I reminded myself of the wonderful promise in Matthew 6:33, "Seek ye first the kingdom of God, and his righteousness; and all these things shall be added unto you." I then prayed, reminding the Lord of His promise.

"Lord, you know I have a family to provide for, bills to pay, gasoline to buy, and now because I love You and want to please and obey You, I have no earthly income. I just quit my job. I am fully trusting in Your promise to supply all our needs because I am obeying You and putting You first. You have promised to take care of us."

I walked all over Cincinnati, looking for another place to work, but none were available.

Our son Philip had eczema; we needed to buy soybean milk for his formula. We had no money, so I felt I should search everywhere in the house for the price of one can, forty-five cents.

I searched under the linoleum floors and found some coins. I searched the sides of the easy chairs and found a few more coins. I went to the car and found a few coins that had fallen out of my pockets when we were not so poor. Still, I didn't have enough money for one can of milk.

The Lord reminded me of the jugs for which I had to pay a deposit when I bought milk. I counted them and it made exactly what I lacked for the soybean milk. I went to the store, happily thanking God for helping me find enough money. When I returned home, my wife met me at the door and excitedly told me we got a check in the mail from someone.

I was out of work for over a month and God so wonderfully supplied all our needs in various ways. We never once shared our need with anyone except the Lord.

We learned from this valuable experience that we could trust God in every circumstance of life to supply our needs. This prepared us for trusting Him throughout our ministry, while pastoring churches with very little income (or none at all) and later as missionaries in Mexico for almost forty years.

Nehemiah's Crisis

In the first verses of the book of Nehemiah we learn where he was when his crisis began. "I was in Shushan the palace." He was faithfully doing his job, far from his beloved Jerusalem, when travelers returned from a long trip.

Permit me to imagine the conversation that might have occurred when Nehemiah found his brother leaning against the palace wall that day.

"Hanani! You're here! How are the people in Jerusalem? Are they thriving?"

Hanani hung his head. "I'm afraid the news is grim, Nehemiah. The remnant at home is suffering and humiliated. After our enemies took away our ancestors, their army broke down Jerusalem's walls and burned the city gates. Those living there now are vulnerable to attacks from wild animals and marauding bands of thieves. Some have even moved to the countryside on the outskirts of Jerusalem. They're afraid another foreign army will come and take more people captive."

This information had a heavy effect on Nehemiah. He sat down and began to weep and fast for his beloved city. Fasting and mourning were never easy to hide from the king. A court attendant had to be easy on the eyes, smiling and upbeat in the presence of his monarch. The idea was to make him think being his servant was the happiest job on earth.

This servant of God started to pray. He wanted to see his beloved city protected from those who would harm her residents. It was a crisis because there was no foreseeable way to make it happen.

Though Nehemiah worked in a palace, he was not blinded by busyness. He could have dismissed the problem as belonging to someone else. Instead, he took a personal interest in it and chose to become involved. This servant didn't blame his people for their circumstances. As one pastor said, "Before he had the chance to turn bitter, he went to God with the need. Before opening his mouth and exposing his heart to his boss, colleagues, or friends, he cried out, 'O Lord God of heaven, the great and terrible (majestic) God'" (Nehemiah 1:5).

Nehemiah's first wise insight was to back off and bathe challenging circumstances in prayer.

Let's consider the structure of Nehemiah's prayer. Chapter one, verses five through eleven provide an excellent model for praying through challenging circumstances.

1. Praise (verse five)

2. Confession (verses six and seven)

3. Reminding God of His promises (verses eight–ten)

4. Submitting a petition (verse eleven)[5]

Prayer Changed Great Britain

Through the ages, God has answered prayers in unique ways. Fast forward from the fifth century before Christ to eighteenth century England. Author Eric Metaxas' book Amazing Grace gives an eye-opening description of that country and culture. Let's observe what happened when people prayed in the day of John and Charles Wesley, founders of the Methodist movement.

> Entirely surprising to most of us, life in eighteenth-century Britain was particularly brutal, decadent, violent, and vulgar. Slavery was only the worst of a host of societal evils that included epidemic alcoholism, child prostitution, child labor, frequent public executions for petty crimes, public dissections and burnings of executed criminals, and unspeakable public cruelty to animals [6] No less than 25 percent of all unmarried women in London were prostitutes. There were brothels that exclusively offered the services of girls under fourteen, and the average age of a prostitute in London during those years was sixteen.[7]

Alcoholism was so rampant in that era that drinking establishments had steps beside the bar, enabling children to order liquor.

The early Methodists fasted and prayed two days a week, from morning until late afternoon. Their praying yielded results. Sinners were delivered from addictions and lives were changed. The praying Methodists turned Great Britain upside down at a time of her lowest moral ebb. Some have credited the Wesleyan revival movement as the means by which England avoided the same kind of bloody revolution France experienced later in that century. The early Methodists added good works to their prayers and established soup kitchens, orphanages, and asylums for destitute people. Shortly after John Wesley died, William Wilberforce succeeded in getting slavery abolished in Great Britain and her colonies.

Kentucky Outlaws Transformed by Prayer

If you've never heard of the Cane Ridge revival in Kentucky, you've missed an important part of American church history. The backstory below helps us understand the significance of this unusual move of God, as people prayed about problems in their difficult culture.

A wave of settlers arrived in Kentucky in the late 1700s and early 1800s. Most were eager to acquire land. Unfortunately, others were eager to acquire lawless living. The western part of the state became a haven for outlaws and criminals. Murderers, horse thieves, and counterfeiters took over the area, with no one to enforce the laws.

The few Christians living in Kentucky at that time became alarmed at the low moral conditions in Logan County. Circuit-riding preacher James McGready challenged three tiny churches to fast and pray each Saturday night and Sunday morning, as well as the third Saturday of each month, asking God to send conviction of sin and genuine revival. At first, conditions became worse. McGready coached them to keep praying.

A Year of Fasting and Prayer Yields Results

The next year, pastors held a customary quarterly meeting in a clearing in the woods of Logan County. Amazingly, 10,000 people showed up! *Lexington, the nearest town, had a population of only 1800.*[8] At that meeting, hardened criminals bowed their knees in repentance and cried to God for mercy. Prayer and fasting worked!

News of this great awakening spread like wildfire. In fact, it spread to Bourbon County, where Rev. Barton Stone urged *his* people to fast and pray like those in Logan County. The small band of Christians under Stone's leadership agreed and began in earnest.

Around 1800, a year after the great move of God in Logan County, Pastor Stone scheduled a weekend camp meeting in the woods of Bourbon County. People were amazed when 25,000 settlers arrived, prepared to watch God move on sinners in answer to their prayers. Not deterred by inconvenience, most traveled the hills of Kentucky by horses and wagons, carrying food and bedding to last for several days.

Scoffers came also, prepared to break up the meetings with drunken revelry. God moved mightily in those services, in answer to the fervent prayer petitions of God's people. Sinners fell to the ground, crying to God for mercy. And the outlaws who blasphemed and proudly claimed they would never partake in such tomfoolery, were stricken down with conviction as the words came out of their mouths. It's noteworthy that this great move of God crossed denominational lines. Presbyterians, Methodists, and Baptists *all* rejoiced as the God of heaven answered prayer.

This second Great Awakening in America resulted in a remarkable change in Kentucky's culture. The area lost its reputation as an outlaw stronghold, while communities of believers flourished. Both the Baptist and Methodist memberships swelled to ten thousand people in the next few years. The Presbyterian church rolls also increased significantly.[9]

Skeptics were silenced when perhaps the greatest skeptic of all, Dr. George Baxter, of Virginia, traveled personally to Kentucky to see for himself. He published his astounding finding in the *Connecticut Evangelical Magazine*, and included these words: "I found Kentucky, to appearance, the most moral place I had ever seen. A profane expression was hardly ever heard. A religious awe seemed to pervade the country."[10]

The Hebrides Revival

The Hebrides (HEB-ruh-deez) revival in Scotland is another example of fervent prayer moving the heart and hand of God from 1949 to 1952. Two women, one eighty-two and the other eighty-four, were troubled when the young people on their island showed no interest in attending church. Despite one woman being blind and the other crippled with arthritis, these siblings agreed to pray twice a week from 10:00 at night until 2:00 or 3:00 in the morning, asking God to move on the hearts of people in their community. At the same time, men who were officers of their church met in a barn and prayed through the night twice a week for about five weeks.[11]

Results were electrifying. A spirit of conviction for sin settled down on the community. Farmers stopped their work in the fields, fell on their knees, and cried to God for mercy. Weavers stopped their looms and did the same. Without any announcement of special meetings, young and old alike flocked to the church to seek the face of God. Places of ill repute closed; people paid their debts; young people gave themselves to full-time Christian service.[12]

Critics attributed the great revival to emotionalism. Their argument proved unfounded when curious men returned to the Hebrides islands years later to check on the state of the church. They found the retention rate remarkably high. Those who had become Christians in the revival remained true to their conversion. *That* is the mark of true revival.

One more point. While it's important for pastors to pray, it is vital for those in the pews (meaning staff, elders, and members who attend) to join them. The story below illustrates this beautifully.

Two elders' wives sat mending their husbands' pants. One of them said to the other, "Poor John, he is so discouraged by his church work. Just the other day, he said that he was considering resigning. It seems like nothing ever goes right for him."

16

The other wife replied, "That's too bad. My husband was saying exactly the opposite. He's been feeling so inspired lately. It seems like he's closer to the Lord than ever."

A heavy silence filled the room as the women continued mending the pants—one the seat and the other the knees (Anonymous).[13]

The Nehemiah Principle

Let's consider what Nehemiah gained by petitioning God *first* before deciding on a course of action.

1. It made him wait and therefore, grow in patience.
2. It cleared his vision.
3. It quieted his heart.
4. It activated his faith.[14]

Nehemiah's story reminds us there are times to act immediately and times to tread softly, allowing the Lord to guide in His unique way. This wise man chose the second, as we will see in the next chapter.

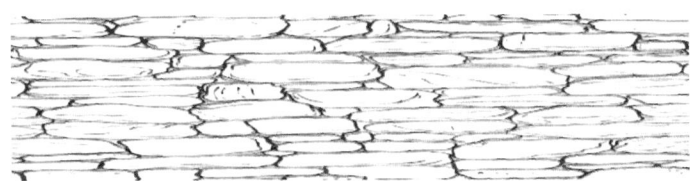

Dear Heavenly Father, if ever I need You, it's now. I don't know how to handle prickly situations that You have allowed to occur. I ask for grace, wisdom, and Christ-like actions and reactions.

Please keep me from gossiping to those who are not part of the solution. And if You want me to wait before taking any action, nudge me when it's time to do something. Teach me how to think like You think and see situations the way You see them. I know You will be sanding the rough edges off my personality through this. Please help me to cooperate with You.

In the name of Jesus Christ our Lord, amen.

CHAPTER THREE

Knocking Knees and Saying Please

Pastor Larry's wife, Janette, experienced a jaw-dropping answer to prayer. Their son, a prodigal, lived far away from home and far from God. Janette prayed for the Lord to send dedicated Christian people across their son's pathway to remind him of his Christian upbringing.

Over 1500 miles away, this PK, running from God, was in a city in Texas to get special job training. He stopped at a restaurant and was astonished to see old friends he had known fifteen years prior, from church camp days in the Midwest. These friends now lived in Delaware and had stopped at the same restaurant on their way to yet another camp in Texas. Before they parted ways, the Delaware friends invited the prodigal to attend the meetings at their destination. Though they didn't know Janette was praying specifically, they became the catalysts to answer her prayer—several hundred miles away from both of their homes.

In the last chapter we noticed prayer and fasting brought results to difficult situations. If you're a pastor with a prickly problem to pray about, four months can seem like an eternity. That's how long Nehemiah brought his challenge to God.

A modern-day pastor faced a challenge in his ministry, as narrated below.

Prayer Built This Church

We found property for a church and were sure this was God's will for us. The location was perfect, right on a busy street. In fact, the city was redoing the street and that would be even better. The next phase was to purchase the property—but with what?

I went to the bank where I kept my own account. After a brief visit, the loan officer smiled politely and said they couldn't help us. I chose another bank. It was a large one and they informed me they did only commercial accounts for big businesses. I made my way to a community bank, thinking they could help us. Our numbers were too few. They were polite but declined to invest in our church.

After exhausting our resources, I slipped into my car at the last place. The Lord spoke to my heart these words: "Could I be your banker?"

Can you imagine my shame! I instantly asked God to forgive me and said I would trust Him for the need.

Before a week passed, my phone rang. The caller on the other end of the line began questioning me about happenings at the church. I told him about wanting to purchase property.

His reply was stunning. "God told me this morning to give you $30,000."

I was shocked. I asked him what the payments would be, and he replied, "No payments. I'm giving it to you."

He then asked how much the owner wanted for the property. "He is asking $36,000," I replied.

My caller's responded, "If God told me $30,000, he will take $30,000."

I met with the owner. He accepted the offer if we would give him a tax donation receipt for the amount. The arrangement was made, and we purchased the property!

We cannot emphasize too much the necessity of bathing special circumstances in prayer, even *fasting* with prayer. How did Nehemiah accomplish this while serving the king? Commentators speculate that cupbearers to the king may have served in shifts, four months at a time.[15] Nehemiah could have used such an arrangement to fast meals.

There are other ways to fast. One can fast *time,* waking up earlier than usual and spending the missed sleep time in prayer. This is helpful for those with physical challenges such as diabetes. Some deny themselves desserts while they pray about a situation. Others give up caffeine (although this can have undesirable side effects). The point is to set aside things you normally do or enjoy, spend time talking to the Lord and listen as He speaks to your heart.

Nehemiah's Example

We saw in previous chapters that those who served ancient kings had to act cheerful to show how delighted they were to be in the monarch's presence. Those in King Artaxerxes' court were no exception. Imagine how difficult it was for a man as heartbroken as Nehemiah to hide his emotions from the one with whom he spent so much time.

Nehemiah was successful for four months, faithfully keeping his petitions before the Orchestrator of the universe, who moves the hearts of kings. Perhaps God gave him a similar thought to the one He gave the writer of Proverbs 21:1: "The king's heart is in the hand of the LORD, as the rivers of water: he turneth it whithersoever he will."

As this faithful servant continued bringing his pleas to God, he confessed his nation's sin of idolatry, though he probably wasn't guilty of it himself. He admitted to the Lord that his people were spiritually disobedient. And after four months, King Artaxerxes noticed his servant-friend's sad countenance.

"Why are you so sad?" asked the king. "This is nothing else but sorrow of heart."

Just like that, God opened an amazing door of opportunity. In Nehemiah 2:2, this Jewish servant tells us he was then "very sore afraid." He had good reason *not t*o anger the king. Monarchs, on a bad day, might end a person's life for petty offenses. However, in today's vernacular, the king probably said next, "So, what do you want from me?"

Like the good leader he was, Nehemiah had planned ahead. However, before answering the king, he did something first. He sent up a silent *arrow prayer*. One commentator expressed it thus, "You cannot acquire this habit of ejaculatory prayer, unless you spend prolonged periods in holy fellowship."[16]

Then this wise servant replied, "Let the king live forever: why should not my countenance be sad, when … the place of my fathers' sepulchers lieth waste." What a wise answer. Nehemiah didn't mention the temple, knowing the heathen people sitting around the king might consider it an affront to their idols. What he *did* know was that sepulchers and other burying places were sacred to *all* religions in the ancient world. The Persian king would be sympathetic to that factor.

You can read the conversation between King Artaxerxes and his servant in Nehemiah 2:2–8. Notice that God had the right people in place at the right time. The queen, sitting beside the king, may have voiced her approval or urged the king to consider the matter.

This wise Jewish servant-leader already had a strategy in mind. When the Lord opened the door of opportunity, Nehemiah walked through it with a well-thought-out plan. In today's language he might have said, "I would like to return to the land of my ancestors' burying place and rebuild the wall around it."

"How long would you be gone?" asked the king. Nehemiah had an answer for that, too. Then he added, "And if it pleases the king, may I have letters of permission to travel through the governors' land beyond the river? And a letter to Asaph, keeper of the king's timber, to request building materials?"

Only prayer and planning could have enabled this servant to make such a bold request. In a matter of minutes, perhaps, the trip was planned, and permission granted. And the reason? Persistent prayer.

In chapter two, verse eight, Nehemiah wisely deflected the credit back to God: "And the king granted me *according to the good hand of my God upon me"* (italics mine).

A Weary Pastor's Answer to Prayer

In our ministry, we experienced the God of heaven orchestrating unusual circumstances in answer to prayer. After my husband pastored small churches for many years, both he and I felt drained. Those who shepherd smaller congregations can attest that ministers and their families fill many roles in addition to the title of pastor. We understood that, yet our failure to take time for rest and relaxation left us with little reserve energy. After many years, we continued to fill our roles in ministry, yet felt emotionally numb. We prayed and asked God what to do. And we waited.

One day, old friends drove ten hours to pay us a visit. What happened on that visit became totally astounding to all of us. While enroute to our house, these friends received a phone call from an acquaintance near their area. The caller said, "Do you know anyone who needs a place to rent? Our tenants just moved from the rental house we own."

Our visiting friends didn't know how badly we needed rest. As their visit progressed in our parsonage, however, they saw we needed a change.

That random phone call led to the perfect place for much-needed physical, emotional, and spiritual renewal, A few months later we found ourselves on sabbatical, living in a quiet community in the country, at the edge of an Old Order Mennonite settlement. It would have been impossible for us to have secured such an ideal place on our own—a three-bedroom house with white carpet and central air conditioning, an attached garage, a shed and barn—all situated on one hundred acres of pastureland. Oh, and the rent? Only $350 a month.

What a spectacular answer to prayer from the God who cares about His weary children. True to His Word, the Lord provided according to

Luke 6:38, "Give, and it shall be given unto you; good measure, pressed down, and shaken together, and running over."

We have seen that intercessory prayer requires commitment and yields results. Let's peek into a volatile situation faced by a young pastor. What does one do when faced with a sticky situation that could polarize an entire congregation? One man chose to follow Nehemiah's example—pray, and wait for God's timing before acting. Below is his story.

Avoiding a Church Split

The phone rang. It was one of our church's single moms who asked if we could come; she had something to tell us. As soon as possible we knocked on her door.

She shared a story about the inappropriate actions of one of our main board members toward her. He had not touched her, but his conversation included several inappropriate questions of a sexual nature. She wanted me to confront him. I assured her I would but only as the Holy Spirit led me. I told her I would remain friendly with him but not to take that as condoning his actions. I would deal with it in God's timing, not mine.

I begged God for wisdom and direction. This man ran the board; everyone voted *with* him, never *against* him on any issue. I understood her complaint but also understood what I was up against as well.

An unwise action on my part would split the church wide open.

The only answer I could sense from God was, *"Give him enough rope; he will hang himself."* Time continued to tick by.

Another phone call came, same thing. My board member exhibited sexually inappropriate actions and words to another woman in our church. This lady just shared her story over the phone. I gave her the same answer I had given the other woman several months before, "Please be assured I will deal with this as the Holy Spirit leads me."

God gave me the same response, "Give him enough rope; he'll hang himself."

I was itching to go confront him, but God continued to hold me back.

I was weary of his opposing everything I brought to the floor in our monthly board meetings. I knew what he was doing; he still ran things. I was about to react humanly, but God said, *Be patient. He's going to hang himself."*

During this time, our church scheduled the annual business meeting and election of officers. This man *always* got elected to the church board on the first ballot.

Before the meeting, there was another phone call. A dear old saint who also was on the board asked, "Pastor, do you know about (she named this man)?"

"What about him?"

"You either know or you don't know." No story, no description, just a question.

Yes," I admitted. "I know."

"I thought you did." She continued, "You know he shouldn't be on the board, don't you?" I said that we couldn't politic him off; that would not be right. Her answer was, "No, but we can pray him off!" I agreed. She continued, "Will you covenant with me that God will keep him from being elected?"

From my heart I answered, "Yes."

Many prayer requests boil down to a chance to spread gossip. Not this one. Other than the man's name, my caller never discussed his offense. There was only the agreement to covenant in prayer. Nothing else, no details, no innuendos were discussed. I had no further discussions about it with her or anyone else during the two weeks before the vote.

The church business meeting arrived, and the man was nominated as expected. Then, paper ballots were passed out to be marked *yes* or *no*. When the votes were counted, the man in question was not reelected. None but the dear old saint had spoken to me about this issue from his first infraction over a year before. Gossip didn't remove this man. God did!

Following the meeting, another board member blustered into my office.

"All right, preacher, what's going on? He's always elected on the first ballot. He didn't get a smell tonight!"

I explained there was something going on, and in good time I would fill him in. The time was not right to tell the story at this point. The board member was not happy but accepted my answer.

Later, I received a phone call from the offender's wife. He had repeated his performance again, on her sister this time. She asked if I would be at their house when he came home from work. I was there, she and her sister and me. He had hung himself (not literally, of course). In that encounter, the issue was brought to the light, and he asked forgiveness.

It was over. Two long years I waited and followed God's directions.[17]

In God's time, I served not as the confronter; I was the referee. The church remained intact, and the problem was handled privately. While I have no statistics to prove my observation, experience has shown that church splits often are created by the pastor's unwise handling. God tells us to seek wisdom. Seek understanding. It's God's way.

The Nehemiah Principle

While this young pastor kept his volatile church situation before the Lord in prayer, God was teaching him to wait for the right time and place to act. Rushing in with a steamroller approach would have caused the weak sheep under his care to scatter, and many who didn't know all the facts probably would have taken sides. Fortunately, he waited.

What about Nehemiah? He had asked the king's assistance for a monumental task—traveling to a ransacked city to rebuild her walls. This wise leader kept his petitions before the God of heaven and waited patiently. He utilized an arrow prayer or a breath prayer with confidence, knowing he had been petitioning God many quiet moments prior to this.

Famous preacher Charles Spurgeon said, "Prayer pulls the rope below and the great bell rings above in the ears of God. Some scarcely stir the bell, for they pray so languidly. Others give but an occasional pluck at the rope. But he who wins with heaven is the man who grasps the rope boldly and pulls continuously, with all his might."[18]

What monumental task lies before you, pastor? You can count on God's support when you know it is his will.

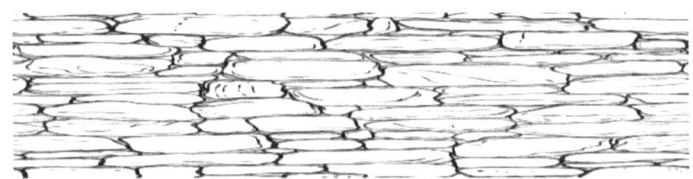

Dear Heavenly Father, the task before me seems impossible. I know, however, that You specialize in things that look impossible. Please make a way where there is no way. I ask, Lord, that You keep my eyes and heart alert for opportunities. And while I'm praying about it, I benefit from learning more about Your unique ways. I love you, Lord. In Christ's name, amen.

CHAPTER FOUR

Shot by Friendly Fire

One of the most disheartening situations a pastor faces is figuratively being shot in the back by people who misunderstand his mission and motives.

Joe pastored a small church. He and his wife, Patty, felt fortunate to have Scott, an old friend of their family, on the board of elders. Scott and his wife, Sue, spent many happy hours with the pastor and his wife. Their children were similar ages, and they all enjoyed fellowship together on Joe's days off. Patty and Sue exchanged frequent phone calls, and shared blessings and burdens.

Pastor Joe and Patty were thrilled when he made a hospital visit to a former prostitute and saw genuine repentance on her part. This woman's radical transformation impressed her extended family so much that they expressed interest in attending Joe's church.

The new convert's amazing transformation also had an electrifying effect on established church members. Formerly lukewarm attendees caught the sparks from her spiritual fire and began digging deeper into their own spiritual conditions. To the pastor's delight, it was the beginning of true revival, not just a series of special services *called* revival.

As often happens, when God moves in wonderful ways, trouble follows. Joe and Patty naturally assumed that the whole congregation would be thrilled with the move of God on their little flock. You can imagine their shock when just the opposite happened.

Shortly after God moved in promising ways, Pastor Joe received unexpected news. *The board demanded his resignation.* This was sudden and felt like a punch in the stomach.

Scott and Sue, whom they trusted as friends, were the strongest instigators, spreading malicious gossip about the pastor's family based on evil surmising. None of it was true. Joe's explanations fell on deaf ears. The board firmly declared he must take his family and leave, with no severance pay, and no farewell service. Puzzled and sorrowful, Pastor Joe and Patty left their beloved place of service in the beginning of what could have been churchwide spiritual renewal.

The church never recovered; sympathetic parishioners found other places to worship. The relationship between former friends never recovered either.

Three Men In Important Positions, Three Sources Of Trouble

Nehemiah 2:10 pulls back the curtain on our man's first hint of trouble. He had the king's approval for his building project; he had the materials. He also had tremendous opposition from those in important positions: Sanballat, Tobiah, and Geshem.

A little historical background: Many years before Nehemiah's time, Israelites lost their national identity by absorbing practices of the heathen nations around them. Let's look at the way the sacred writer describes Israel's sins. You can read about it in II Kings 17:15-17.

1. Rejecting God's statutes and covenant, given through Moses

2. Following their heathen neighbors' sinful practices

3. Making molten idols, such as two calves, to worship

4. Using groves of trees for immoral, deviant practices

5. Worshipping the sun, moon, stars, and planets

6. Serving Baal (the sun god), a filthy idol connected with sexual immorality

7. Causing their children to pass through the fire to please heathen idols

8. Using divination and enchantments (consulting wizards
   and fortune tellers)

Simply put, the Israelites departed from the ways God had shown their ancestors to live. Though the Lord God still loved His people, he chose to discipline them by scattering them among wicked nations. This set the stage for Nehemiah's dilemma: opposition to his leadership.

You may have learned in Sunday school, as I did, that the Samaritans and the Jewish people despised one another. I always wondered why, until I researched II Kings 17:24. After Assyria conquered the northern kingdom of Israel in 721 B.C., Assyria's king repopulated Samaria (near the center of the land mass we know as Israel) with colonists from heathen nations. Those people intermarried with the Jewish people and established a new ethnic group called Samaritans.[19]

To a Jewish person, this was the ultimate insult. When their otherwise pure bloodlines became polluted by those they considered half-breeds, the Jewish people viewed their part-Jewish, part-Gentile neighbors with disgust. Families hoping to bring forth the coming Messiah thought God wouldn't send his Son through a polluted genealogy. So, Samaria, a hub of cross-pollinated people, became a place of loathing.[20]

Into this arena stepped Sanballat, governor of Samaria. Sanballat was a Babylonian name; he also was called the Horonite. Commentators believe he was from Beth-horon, about eighteen miles northwest of Jerusalem—close enough to have an interest in Jerusalem's politics.[21] He may have felt Nehemiah was a threat to his leadership if he hoped to become the governor of Jerusalem. This was our first hint that jealousy was about to rear its ugly head.

Sanballat apparently worshipped Israel's God, but added pagan worship introduced by the Assyrian colonists. His daughter married into the Jewish high priest's family, causing another sticky situation. (Nehemiah had an interesting confrontation with Sanballat's son-in-law, but we'll read about that in chapter twelve.) In short, Sanballat represented mixing pagan lineage and worship with pure Jewish bloodlines and worship.

The second man who gave Nehemiah problems was Tobiah, also called "the servant, the Ammonite." Biblical history tells us the Ammonites descended from Ammon, son of Lot by his incestuous relationship with his youngest daughter. Although Ammonites were cousins of the Israelites, they remained bitter enemies.[22]

Ammonites were notorious for being cruel and idolatrous; they worshipped the idols Milcom and Molech and offered human sacrifices. In Deuteronomy 23:3, God commanded the Israelites not to deal with them to avoid corruption from their evil ways.[23]

Tobiah is thought to have been a freed slave, elevated to the office of district magistrate. To complicate matters, he married a Jewish woman, a relationship that allowed him inside scoop on Jewish gossip. This factor alone was a formula for disaster.

Geshem, another source of trouble, is simply called "the Arabian." Although the Bible doesn't mention this man elsewhere, modern-day scholars think he may have been a chief of the Kedar, a nomadic or Bedouin tribe.[24]

Nehemiah's problem with dissenters mirrors one that sometimes plagues pastors today: jealous onlookers feeling threatened by a good work. In fact, "It grieved them exceedingly that there was come a man to seek the welfare of the children of Israel" (Nehemiah. 2:10).

The following section contains one longtime pastor's reflections on hindrances to the work of the Lord:

I Cannot Come Down

Satan always has had his Sanballets and Tobiahs. Even in the church age there are those whom the enemy sends around to hinder the work of God. The devil uses three distinct tools to try to stop or hinder God's work. They are *distractions, diversions,* and *divisions.*

Distractions can be anything that prevents a person from giving full attention to a task. I would relate distractions to annoyances, irritations, and little frustrations. Life is full of these and no doubt the enemy of our souls delights in magnifying them, trying to use them to hinder the work and walk of the believer. You will notice the enemies of Nehemiah wasted no time in starting the distractions, by laughing at and making fun of the Jewish workers.

Diversions include the act of turning something or someone aside from its intended course. It implies a more serious threat. The skeptics and critics always will have something negative to say, except "Don't come down; you're doing a great work." Get your calling and commission from God and then don't deviate from it until God releases you.

Divisions are more demanding and require a determined course of action on our part to not let them affect us. In Nehemiah's case, laughter turned to open mockery, to discourage the workers.

A well-known Christian speaker once said that in debate training, his professor advised, "If you don't have a strong argument, try attacking your opponent's." Sanballat and Tobiah seemed to be masters of this concept.

A friend related this story about one church that narrowly escaped division that would have destroyed a good man's reputation.

The pastor of a small church provided free transportation to needy persons who were unable to drive to services themselves. Once, after a church service, he drove a woman back to her home. One of his members happened to be going the same way for a few miles, and followed in her car. From her vantage point, it looked as though the pastor's passenger snuggled beside him, and he had his arm around her. Shocked, the observer was ready to report this to church officials.

Then, the pastor made a right-hand turn, and the offended member saw what she had missed. The passenger actually sat in the *back* seat, while the pastor rested his arm on the back of the *front* seat. From a distance, it looked as though he was being morally loose. If this observer had not seen the actual situation a few moments later, imagine the diversion and division that would have occurred when a good minister faced false charges, based on what someone thought she saw.

One experienced pastor recounted a situation where his life was in danger after moving to a new charge. Here is the story in his own words.

Pastor Jared's Deliverance from His Sanballat

As a leader, it is sometimes hard to hear churches have deteriorated almost beyond repair, especially those places that are dear. Our ministry experience included such a time when a church was spiritually torn to the point of closing. In fact, it had been closed for many months. The conference sent us to this place to try to bring it back to life.

When we visited, only one family wanted the church to open again. We could not get into the building, so I climbed through a window. We held a service that weekend and began to make plans to move to the community as soon as possible. One thing possibly would stand in the way: the former pastor. When this person heard the church was reopened, here came "Sanballat," with great indignation that I would have the nerve to open the church again. After all it was "their" church.

The introduction was not very favorable. Sanballat was not pleased and fought the worship times. This former pastor was visible at every service and tried to talk among the few people who came about my daring to come and take over the church without their consent. They were not finished pastoring there.

We had to go around the small community, paying bills made in the name of the church: clothing and furniture for their "parsonage" home.

But with God's help, we accomplished clearing the church's reputation. We made headway in the community and people began attending.

Sanballat Was Not Finished

This former pastor gave us a call one night and said we had stolen the church from them. I explained that the conference had sent us there. Sanballat said they would get a hit man to take care of the conference leader. And a group of men who supported them would come to church, take me outside and beat me up. Of course, we prayed and sought God's will about the situation.

Sunday, here they came, about thirty of them, and sat down. Our church people were afraid and ready to leave. I told them God had everything under control and we should let Him handle the situation. We would just reverse Sunday school and the preaching service.

The vigilante committee was not expecting that.

Our song leader came to the front to lead the singing but was trembling so hard it was nearly impossible to finish. We continued with the usual preliminaries, and then I got up to preach.

God certainly came on the scene and helped this lowly servant preach an anointed message. During the preaching, the "hit men" began to get up and leave one by one, until there were only about ten of them left.

When I finished preaching, I opened the altar for anyone who wanted to pray. Oh, how God was moving in our midst! Two of the hit men came to the altar and were gloriously saved from their sins. The rest of them slipped out the door while we were praying with seekers at the altar.

What a wonderful time we had when these men prayed through to victory. Sanballat was speechless and had to leave the church defeated.

The men who came to the altar became our good friends and helped in the church afterward. They refused to speak to Sanballat because they knew they would be fighting against the Lord and His work.

Sanballat was defeated, and God got the glory. The church continued to grow after that, all because a few souls dared to pray and trust God for the outcome.

Now let's view the path Nehemiah took when dealing with those threatened by his leadership. Realizing the opposition before him, this wise leader kept a low profile at first. He sized up the damaged city walls secretly at night. Imagine the clop-clop of his mount's hooves on the silent street as he made mental notes of what he needed to rebuild the crumbled walls. Even the few men who accompanied him probably were puzzled by their leader's sudden bout of insomnia that led to a late-night sightseeing trip.

Of course, I am not suggesting pastors should be covert in all their plans. There is wisdom in consulting counselors. However, in Nehemiah's instance, publishing his plan far ahead of time would have disastrous consequences. So, Nehemiah kept a low profile.
Another pastor contributed the following when asked advice about employing Nehemiah's strategy.

Private Preparation before Public Declaration

A pastor taking up a new assignment told friends and family that when he got to the new church, he was going to "clean house." Of course, he meant dealing with what he perceived to be unresolved problems and the people who fostered them. However, within a short time, church attendance plummeted and he found himself looking for another pastorate. Perhaps the story would have been different had the pastor followed the example of Nehemiah and waited to do his talking until it was talking time.

Wise leaders throughout history have understood and practiced the principle of maintaining plans quietly until a wise time to reveal them. Gideon launched his first offensive at night, when he and ten servants destroyed the local grove dedicated to Baal worship (Judges 6). The Apostle Paul spent three years in obscurity in Arabia before revealing himself to the apostle Peter and later, to James, the Lord's brother. Jesus employed secrecy at crucial junctures of his earthly ministry, including a conversation with Nicodemus under cloak of night.

Michael was a new pastor with a problem many ministers face eventually: resistance to their leadership. Here is his account of the way God led him through a difficult situation.

How Do I Get These People to Follow?

Leadership, with its many facets, varying approaches, and differing objectives has one common denominator at its core: *influence*. Every leader is tasked with the responsibility of affecting others in such a way that they are compelled to follow him or her in a specific undertaking.

For Nehemiah, the task at hand was the erection of the Jerusalem wall. God had converted the cupbearer into a construction foreman. Nehemiah may or may not have been a man of great credentials, but he was a man of deep conviction and so must be every individual who takes the helm in the attempt to lead others. Leadership can prove extremely difficult, but it remains equally simple; *go in the direction God has ordained and do so in such a convincing way that others will follow.*

The work of rebuilding Jerusalem's walls was unquestionably God's agenda. He had plucked Nehemiah from the comforts of familiarity, provided miraculously, and had given him favor with his brethren. By the fourth chapter of Nehemiah, the endeavor was well underway. "The wall was joined together unto the half thereof for the people had a mind to work" (Nehemiah 4:6).

This progress, however, had not come without persecution (it seldom does). Nehemiah and his workers faced fierce fury from Sanballat, Tobiah, and others (Nehemiah 4:1, 7). The threats of these dissenters seemed a weightier matter than the rubble the bearers had to carry (v. 10). As fear increased, strength decreased, and leadership became imperative.

Many years ago, while pastoring a growing congregation, I was contacted by the president of a local denomination. He had a church that lay on the brink of closure, some forty miles from my primary pastorate. He asked if I would be willing to travel the distance, add two services to my weekly schedule, and see if the work could be rejuvenated.

When I arrived that first Sunday, I found a large building nestled in a lonely curve in the middle of a rural community. Its brick front faced the roadway and offered a touch of aesthetic improvement over cinder block sides. A large set of steps invited one to enter. Inside I found empty wooden pews resting on a solid oak floor, surrounded by white plaster walls. There were three in attendance, two men and one lady, each near eighty years of age.

I have had the privilege of preaching to four and to fourteen thousand. It takes the same anointing to do either. That morning, I settled somewhere in between mentally and preached as if it were camp meeting or an international crusade. God encouraged their hungry hearts and mine also. They asked if I would return, and I agreed.

It was the beginning of a long and loving relationship. But it wasn't always that way.

During my time there, we had much to do. Like the walls of Jerusalem, the church was in disarray. Years of neglect marked every aspect of the work. Facilities were dilapidated; the congregation was discouraged; and the community had determined the effort was but a memory.

After six months I was asked to pastor. Technically, it was not permitted under the protocol of the denomination due to my other appointment. I considered nevertheless, my commitment hinging on another: that the budding congregation would fully support improvement efforts, which I felt were crucial for going forward.

In the months that followed, we restored the foundation, added a new roof, steeple, and sign, and spent countless hours cleaning areas and discarding debris. The congregation grew and drew a fresh breath. This wall, like Nehemiah's, was being built. Then came opposition.

The strange thing about opposition is that it's not always an external issue.

Some of the greatest resistance a leader must rise above comes from within. In the case of Nehemiah, external foes had generated fear that threatened to cripple the work, but in the case of many leaders (and especially pastors) it is friends, family, or parishioners who create the very fear they must overcome.

Success can be nearly as scary as failure. It is marked by change and demands that people change with it. This can be difficult. Most people fear the unknown. Success is sometimes seen as merely a departure from that to which one has grown accustomed. It is therefore less predictable, less manageable, and less desirable.

In Nehemiah's case, the wall of Jerusalem was coming together. The vision was materializing. Yet, the voices of opposition were drowning out the determination of the people. Nehemiah did what every leader must do in such a situation; he looked to the greatest Leader. He penned, "Nevertheless we made our prayer unto our God" (Nehemiah 4:9a).

Every leader must learn to follow. Everyone who hopes to have influence among men must be primarily influenced by the One who is sovereign over men.

By focusing on the One who called him to the work, Nehemiah found courage. He then was able to serve as a catalyst of courage among his brethren (v. 14). With a tool in one hand and a weapon in the other (v. 17), they pressed ahead. Some would focus on security (vv. 13, 16), but all would play a part. If the wall were to be built, it would be built only by their working together.

Back to my story. We had cleaned out a long-forgotten basement at the newly assumed pastorate and established a storage area for those few things that managed to avoid the landfill. We placed decorations, memorabilia, and supplies in an orderly fashion on shelves. Over a year had passed in the process and I was confident we were moving in the right direction.

One day, I noticed a small shelf on the platform that had become a catchall. I decided to go through the contents and place anything useful in a more permanent location. Among the items was a tarnished communion set, which I stored in the basement.

The following Sunday I was met by the church boss.

He was an elderly gentleman, the dominating voice of the congregation Brother Church Boss teemed with trepidation. This man informed me it was bordering on blasphemy to take something as sacred as the communion set to the nasty quarters of the basement. I tried explaining the situation, yet he responded with more indignation.

Realizing he was having none of it, I took another approach. "If the communion set is such a sacred item, why have we neglected the sacrament?"

He assured me the church believed in such means of grace and had often participated in the Lord's Supper. I saw an opportunity, so I scheduled a communion service for the following Sunday. He consented.

The following week all was in place. Anger subsided; everyone was looking forward to the event. We arranged the communion set ceremoniously for the larger-than-usual crowd. After the event, I announced that my tradition often included the washing of feet in such a service, and we were prepared to do so.

I dismissed ladies to another portion of the church and invited men to the front. We poured water into a basin and placed a towel beside it, as men removed their shoes and socks. He sat silently on the front pew, leaning on crutches to stable his feeble frame.

Each of the others took part, and soon we came to him. He quickly explained that he too had participated in such ceremonies many times before, but time had deteriorated his ability. He could no longer even bend over to remove his own shoes.

I immediately saw an opportunity: to lead, to serve, to relieve fears.

I knelt before him, removed his shoes and socks, rolled up his trousers, and began to wash his feet. He wept. It was a turning point in my leadership. He would never question my decisions again. *He looked beyond actions and saw attitude. It influenced him.*

Nehemiah bound his people together and the church boss and I did the same. Fear had been put to flight. For Nehemiah, it took an act of bravery. For me, it was an act of humility. The outcome, however, was the same; the work would go forward through unity.

Every leader is tasked with the daunting responsibility of influencing others to follow their leadership, to join them in the task. John Maxwell summarizes, "If you think you are leading and no one is following, you are simply taking a walk."

Nehemiah's Naysayers

Nehemiah's enemies tried common tactics to hinder the work. They used ridicule and scorn. "Will ye rebel against the king?" They tried to get this godly man to doubt his calling, his loyalty to the king. A common saying, attributed to many famous people, states, "A lie can travel halfway around the world while the truth is putting on its shoes."

Does this sound familiar, pastor? *"Who does he think he is, anyway?"* Nehemiah was one step ahead of his enemies with a wise reply. First, he assured his detractors that the God of heaven would give His people success. Then, he reminded them of something else. "Ye have no portion, nor right, nor memorial, in Jerusalem" (Nehemiah. 2:20). He told them they lacked true relationship with his people. It was an honor to be a citizen of Jerusalem. They couldn't claim that privilege.

If that sounds abrupt, consider the alternative. Nehemiah's commission came from God. Caving in to threats and sarcasm from his enemies would have extinguished all hope his fellow citizens had of seeing their beloved city restored to a safe sanctuary.

The Nehemiah Principle

As a student of human nature, Nehemiah knew the people of Jerusalem needed two things before the project started:

1. The assurance of the king's approval
2. A reminder of the way God had prospered His work to that point

Because this godly leader had immersed this plan in much prayer and careful thought, the people readily agreed.

The next time critics attack your actions, take it to prayer. With a God-given plan in mind, lend little time to the naysayers. Keep facing forward but expect criticism from those who may not know the whole situation.

One pastor wrote, "After almost forty years in full-time ministry, I have learned to quit chasing the false accusations, the sordid rumors, and the threats by those who would oppose the work of God. Stay at your post of duty, faithful Christian, and refuse to give the enemies of God the pleasure of your coming down!"

Those who accomplish anything for God's kingdom know that opposition is inevitable. That's Satan's business. God will give you courage for the asking.

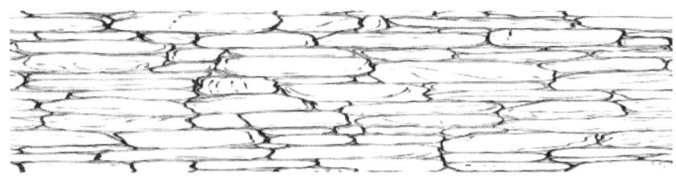

Dear Father in Heaven, You see the attacks that have come my way from those I thought were my friends. It hurts, of course, but Your Son also was misunderstood. Please give me strength of character to leave these misunderstandings with You. I take my marching orders from Christ, the captain of my salvation. Lead on!

CHAPTER FIVE

Motivation and Infiltration

Experience has taught us that when God calls people to do a task, he provides whatever skills are necessary. Nehemiah enlisted the help of ordinary laymen and women in rebuilding the crumbled walls of Jerusalem. As a leader, he probably acquired skills he may not have possessed previously, such as laboring in heavy construction. His leadership secret? Motivating people to work *with* him, not *for* him.

Coach and Team Player

One of the most industrious persons we observed in leadership was the wife of a camp president. Each year prior to this family event, she organized girls and women in their small church to clean rooms that the campers would occupy. This was no ordinary "lick-and-a-promise" cleaning. Working alongside the girls, she vacuumed mattresses, washed walls, windows, and doorframes, even cleaned ceiling light fixtures. Her success lay in the fact that she used *we* instead of *you* to get the work done. Like Nehemiah, she was both coach and team player.

If you had visited Nehemiah's job site during the wall-building project, you wouldn't have found him sitting under a tent, sipping lemonade. Instead, he walked among the workers, encouraging, giving advice, and keeping watch for the enemy. He probably picked up a tool at times to demonstrate wall building to novices.

There *were* novices, of course. The Biblical record tells us persons from all walks of life worked alongside each other: farmers, priests, goldsmiths, merchants, women, and even the governors' sons. It was backbreaking, callous-making work. Nehemiah's dedication to the task was so contagious that men from Jericho, over twenty-two miles away, came to help.

One of the most striking instances of God providing skills to the unskilled occurred during a pastorate in the Midwest. You can read this pastor's wife's narrative below.

Celestial Piano Lessons

Our church piano player was every song leader's dream. Ron could play anything in any key, with or without written music. His complex chords and creative progressions set a worshipful tone for congregational singing. If someone suddenly broke into song, this virtuoso's fingers instantly picked up the tune and provided heart-warming accompaniment.

Soloists appreciated Ron's professional accompaniment. His unique method enhanced their sometimes-amateur voices and made them appear several notches above their skill level.

As an accompanist on the church organ, I appreciated the privilege of lending my limited skill to Ron's stellar technique. Perhaps if I kept the volume down, people scarcely would notice my lack.

To our chagrin, this musical prodigy moved to another state, leaving a huge void in the worship services. The church board elected me to fill his place. Sometimes the pastor's wife is drafted to fill vacancies in places where she doesn't feel comfortable. This was one of those places.

It was humiliating in the beginning. A year of secular college piano lessons hadn't prepared me to arrange chords and progressions, to lend dignity to majestic hymns, and exuberance to lilting gospel tunes. Though no one complained, I felt like a child playing "Chopsticks" for a crowd at Carnegie Hall.

This went on for some time. One day, sitting at the ebony grand piano in the empty sanctuary, I prayed a simple prayer. "Lord, the worship service isn't the same without Ron's beautiful music. Could You teach me to play better than I know how, so the service will be a blessing?"

God answered my prayer progressively. From that time onward, when I played hymns for worship, I noticed a gradual change. If I tried to play simple chords that I knew, my fingers hit more complex ones, which previously I had struggled to locate. Then, I applied these to other songs. Over a span of months God changed my piano technique in answer to that simple prayer. We received a blessing as beautiful, anointed music filled the church once more.

Our youth leader approached me after several weeks and said, "I notice your piano playing is different than it used to be." Yes, it was. Thank you, Lord![25]

Lack of Enthusiastic Workers

As with some community projects, not everyone was excited about Nehemiah's work. Some of the nobles from Tekoa, about ten miles away, had the attitude, "Here am I; send my brother," so their humble townspeople took up the slack when their own sections were completed. Any trailblazer who has gotten a good work off the ground will vouch that God has yet to shape the leader who has 100% cooperation.

Another facet of Nehemiah's leadership was his wisdom in appealing to family ties. He assigned persons to build a section of the wall close to their own home. If you were fortifying a wall against invaders, wouldn't you give particular attention to the area near *your* house?

Since the family is the first institution God created, it makes sense that Satan attacks it the most viciously. And that's why pastors can be blessed or troubled by families—their own and other people's.

Families: Ties That Bind … or Gag

Consider Tom, a pastor who fell out of favor with his church congregation. The reason? He had to confront a hypocritical person with strong family ties to nearly everyone in his small church. Tom's only recourse was to leave; he had offended this person's brother, cousin, parents, and brother-in-law.

What's a pastor to do in that circumstance? Saturating a situation in prayer is the best course of action, before any other takes place. Some ministers find it necessary to leave the work and serve elsewhere, as Tom did. Unfortunately, that leaves the next pastor to face the same issue. Others stay and experience pressure each week as they preach to disgruntled relatives of the one who was removed from office due to a hypocritical life.

Brian, a successful pastor for many years, was happy to write several pages of advice to young ministers and those facing leadership challenges. Below are excerpts of the wisdom he gained through practical experience.

One Pastor's Advice: Build Relationships

Our years of pastoral ministry began just a little later in our lives as I struggled for several years with answering a call to preach. Not surprisingly, I also was struggling with a clear experience of entire sanctification. The last thing I yielded to God was my willingness to surrender my will for His.

That began much effort to prepare for the ministry. I did it the hard way, for now I had the responsibility of a family of four. God miraculously provided a full-time job working three to eleven; thus, I was able to attend Bible college part-time on school days. After four years of that rugged schedule, my wife and I felt the burden to get started in pastoral ministry.

Our first church was a little home missions work in North Carolina. God gave us unusual opportunities to connect with people and gain the approval of the community.

One of the first initiations of acceptance was whether I would eat a raw clam or oyster. (I found that I preferred the oyster over the clam.) Then a group of men took me clamming for a day. Anchoring a boat in the middle of the intercoastal waterway, they handed me a clam rake and showed me how to pull it through the sand in shallow water. They told me to catch all the clams I could, and then they disappeared out of sight for much of the day.

I started raking and soon found a lot of clams amid some seaweed. I was happy when I caught 600 of them—until the men returned.

They took one look and groaned.

I had caught chowder clams, the ones they got the least money for at the dock. I believe I got about six cents per clam. Their nice, small ones yielded about twenty-one cents per clam. Oh well, I still could boast of catching 600 my first day out. Never mind that I had trouble moving my arms for several days. I was accepted by the locals!

The Crooked Baptist

We learned to pray and trust the Lord for the needs we faced. The air conditioner in our bedroom was one need. It would hardly cool anymore; we were getting desperate for relief.

One day a local man stopped outside the parsonage and just blew his truck horn until I went out to see what he wanted. He said he wanted to buy me an air conditioner; could I use one? I jumped into his truck and hours later installed a new air conditioner in our bedroom.

This man called himself a crooked Baptist. He had been an insurance agent who was not always well thought of in the community. I learned to like him despite his reputation.

Our little church could pay me only seventy-five dollars a week, so I worked my painting trade to survive financially. My new friend learned about my skills and soon I was painting just about everything he owned: his boats, as well as the interior of his house. He helped spread the word of my painting skills and I never lacked for jobs. It was great, and I was connecting with the locals.

People came from all over that little fishing village and surrounding communities to see what was going on in the holiness church across the brook. We had some remarkable conversions in those two years of ministry. Some amazing answers to prayer occurred, which built our faith and encouraged our ministry efforts. I did my first baptism in salt water at the harbor and made friends with whom we still connect.

Blessed by a Hurricane

In 1989, when Hurricane Hugo was coming ashore, the local people asked if we were leaving and going inland, since all the other preachers were doing so. They thought it strange that all the men of God would abandon the area at a time like that.

I said we planned to stay. We left our doublewide parsonage, boarded up windows, and settled into our block-constructed church. Then we gathered all the supplies we thought we would need. One of our neighbors gave us a marine radio so we could keep in contact and have a way to call for help. The worst of the storm was expected to hit during the night.

My family of four settled into our makeshift beds and slept most of the night. Thankfully, the storm shifted, and our area did not get the full brunt of it. We escaped with minimal damage, yet gained maximum respect among the people. God was building our faith in Him to see us through the storms of life.

When word got out that we were moving away, the whole community threw a farewell party for us at the Baptist church pavilion.

They cut a hole in the top of a fish box and placed it out for people to give us a financial blessing. We were shocked when we received $1,000 that day! God was meeting our needs.

New Challenges

From there we went into some of our most challenging years of ministry. I took a pastorate in another state, following a pastor who had a sixteen-year tenure.

It was hard for some in the church to accept this inexperienced whippersnapper who handled things so differently than their previous pastor. While many wonderful things happened during our years there, they were quite overshadowed by dealings with differences of opinion, personalities, and outright carnality.

I sought advice from conference leadership, from my dear father, and from the Holy Spirit. Battles raged as I faced some of the darkest days of my life. There were times I questioned my own experience of heart holiness and came close to leaving the ministry altogether. God miraculously sustained us and kept bitterness from creeping into our hearts.

We felt directed to move on to another pastorate where I followed one who had a ten-year tenure as pastor. I began to implement things I had learned from the previous two pastorates, *especially how to deal with strong personalities in church leadership*. We saw amazing growth numerically and had a solid ministry of seventeen years at this church. Honestly, it was like a seventeen-year honeymoon.

Following Another Long-Term Pastor

It was hard to understand when God lifted the burden for that work and challenged us to move on in faith. But that is exactly what we did. We moved to another state and followed a pastor who had a thirty-year tenure. Do you see the pattern? It seemed God wanted me to help churches transition from long-term pastorates. It is not always the easiest.

We thought we had reached our sweet spot in this little country church. We could see us staying in this much slower pace until retirement, but God had other plans. Our "sabbatical" lasted only ten months.

I am not sure why God opened that door for us, but I do not regret walking through it. Yes, it was quite humbling to resign about six months after moving into their parsonage. We knew God had been speaking to us about the next pastorate for some time but had no idea it would open to us so soon. In fact, we were in this out-of-state pastorate only three months when I received a call from the leadership of the church for which God was burdening our hearts.

God helped us to accomplish much during our ten-month pastorate, but the most comforting words I heard were the thank-yous for helping them transition from their previous pastor. I was the buffer who led to a good ministry position for the one serving there now.

Brian's Advice to New Pastors

It is important that you learn to work with what you have. One must be patient and dead to self. Learn to discuss matters with key people in your congregation. Endeavor to get their support and they will help you move forward with things. Work on building relationships and gaining the trust and confidence of the people. It will do much to build momentum for Kingdom building and will contribute to many happy years in a pastorate.

The church I have been serving for nearly ten years has been an amazing journey. The senior pastor before me served for thirty-five years. I have needed all that I learned in each of my previous pastorates.

It is very important that ministers of the gospel be humble servants, ever eager to learn how to love people and work with them. While in this pastorate I have learned to accept some *no* votes in the recall voting. I have learned to deal with an annual pastoral evaluation. Criticism can be a hard pill to swallow, but when given for your ultimate good, it can be a wonderful benefit.

Also, in this present pastorate I have learned that my ideas are not always the best ones. I have discovered what it means to serve in a very demanding work. The number of sermons to preach, people to visit, events to participate in, and office work to get done can be overwhelming. I do not regret putting much effort into preparing sermons, gathering books and sermon helps, and learning how to work with people. I am truly reaping the result of a good work ethic and in putting my all into being the best pastor I can be. It has been a joy to pass along some of the things I have learned to eager ministerial minds.

Our church takes very good care of us in many ways, and the congregation is extremely supportive. I feel very keenly the intense prayers they offer on my behalf. The manifestation of God's presence in our services and upon the ministry efforts of this church is very convincing and refreshing.

My wife has been a special blessing in all our years of marriage and ministry. She shines in so many ways and truly has been my helpmate. Our children and grandchildren are such a blessing to us.

It is my prayer that many more will feel the call to ministry and that they will be honest seekers after God's heart. May they also be eager learners in their own pursuits of preparation to serve.

Infiltration and Discouragement

Sheep don't always appreciate having the shepherd pull burrs out of their wool. It hurts. Likewise, church members don't always love the pastor when he exercises tough love. But it's part of his job to protect his people, just as Nehemiah's job was to protect the residents of Jerusalem.

As in many huge projects, things were going well for Nehemiah when trouble arrived. When the wall was about half as tall as planned, naysayers on the outside began to worry. Their leadership was potentially threatened. Since Sanballat commanded the army of Samaria, some think he may have led them to stand outside the walls of Jerusalem to taunt and intimidate the builders. Thus began his conspiracy to disrupt the work.

There are four ways God's people are attacked when they do a good work.

1. Discouraging sarcasm.
2. Enemies within and without.
3. Disunity within.
4. False accusations.[26]

In Nehemiah 4:1–6, we read of the insults and sarcasm Sanballat heaped on the hard-working Jewish laborers. In today's vernacular he may have said, "Do these feeble Jews think they can build this by themselves? Do they think they can do the job in one day? Look at them! Do they think they can reuse stones from the rubbish pile?"

Tobiah added his own insult, "Yes. Even if they do build their stone wall, it will fall down if a little fox treads on it."

Did you ever notice rebels like to surround themselves with prepackaged supporters?

Nehemiah's response in 4:4 and 4:5 leaves us wondering how this servant of God could pray such a severe prayer against his oppressors. He prayed, "Hear, O our God; for we are despised: and turn their reproach [sometimes translated *criticism*] upon their own head, and give them for a prey in the land of captivity:" He continued his imprecation in the next verse: "And cover not their iniquity, and let not their sin be blotted out from before thee."

Geneva Bible Notes offers this outlook: "Let the plagues declare to the world that they set themselves against you and your Church: that he prays only having respect for God's glory and not for any private affection, or grudge."[27]

There are similar prayers in the psalms. We must remember that Nehemiah's day precluded the gospel era, where Jesus taught his followers to love their enemies. It was this dedicated leader's goal to see his people regain their national identity.

Commentator Matthew Henry observed the following: "Nehemiah had reason to think that the hearts of those sinners were desperately hardened, else he would not have prayed that their sins might never be blotted out."[28]

Jamieson-Fausset-Brown Commentary said, "The imprecations invoked here may seem harsh, cruel, and vindictive; but it must be remembered that Nehemiah and his friends regarded those Samaritan leaders as enemies to the cause of God and therefore *deserving to be visited with heavy judgments*. The prayer, therefore, is to be considered as emanating from the heart in which neither hatred, revenge, nor any inferior passion, but a pious and patriotic zeal for the glory of God and the success of His cause, held that ascendant sway" (italics mine).[29]

Commentator Adam Clarke thought Nehemiah's declarations of God's judgments applied to his enemies' *bodies* and *lives,* not their souls. According to Clarke, the verb tense in the Hebrew "turn their reproach" could be rendered, "*their reproach shall be turned*." And "give them for a prey" could be rendered, "*They shall be given for a prey*."[30] In other words, Nehemiah was wishing for these enemies of God in this life to reap what they sowed. Interesting to note is that this prayer was fulfilled by the Maccabees and their successors.

An Inside Job

If the enemy of your soul can't get to you from the *outside*, he will try an *inside* job.

During the last century, when communist oppression laid a heavy hand on European ministers, several pastors spent time in prison for preaching and practicing their faith. One discouraging tactic their tormentors used was planting supposed "other Christians" in their prison cells to discourage the suffering saints. These decoys, posing as fellow Christians, gathered inside information about other believers. In addition, they suggested the pastors' wives were being unfaithful to their husbands in their absence. *Infiltration* and *discouragement* were their tactics, patterned after both Nehemiah's enemies and Satan, the original oppressor.

Pastor Chris and the Helpful Member

Sherry was the most helpful person in Pastor Chris's church. Her sweet, soft voice, charming smile, and volunteer spirit made it easy for her to become the poster child for the congregation's inner circle, the ones who influenced church decisions and policy.

After several families stopped attending and relationships appeared strained, Pastor Chris and his wife, Barb, suspected some ONE might be responsible.

A clue popped up in a ladies' prayer meeting one night. Barb noticed the group of ladies gossiped maliciously about their "prayer requests" for several minutes, and then spent only a short time praying for them. Sweet little Sherry gossiped the most.

God then gave another clue, which came as a total surprise. One Wednesday evening after church, Barb felt an urge to return to the parsonage to do some sewing in the room overlooking the church parking lot. All the cars were gone except two. One was Sherry's and the other belonged to a woman who had faithfully attended the church for years. The two women held a lengthy conversation in one of the cars. Could Sherry be gossiping again? A short time later, Sherry's confidante from the parking lot stopped attending Chris's church, following the pattern of several others. The clues led down the right trail. Sweet little Sherry was being used by Satan to divide and disrupt a good work. A good church had been split apart by an infiltrator on the inside.

Unfortunately, the church failed to recover from the damage. Several years after Pastor Chris and his family moved away and the membership dwindled significantly, Sherry wrote a weak letter to Chris, apologizing "if" she had ever opposed his ministry.

Pastor Chris knew that the Holy Spirit is faithful and specific when showing us our faults and sins. Thus, when someone feels guilty and issues an apology that begins with "*if* I have done anything wrong," it's often evidence they need to dig deeper. When confessing transgressions, a person needs to specify exactly what their offense was. Naming the wrong can be painful, yet will serve as a deterrent for repeating the action in the future. Humbling oneself is difficult, but necessary to keep unity among believers.

Of course, there are principles to observe in confession of faults and/or sins. One teenage girl in my public school years ago lacked knowledge of proper protocol to confess her sins. She had read the passage in James 5:16, "Confess your faults one to another..." As a result, she wrote a note saying, "Sometimes I lie," and dropped it on the desk of a bewildered classmate. You can imagine the strange impression that made on someone from a secular background. How much better if Jill (not her real name) had confessed to her local church or her pastor, and asked for prayer concerning that issue.

Another important principle regarding confession of faults and sins is that the confession should extend just as far as the sin occurred. In the case of "Sweet Little Sherry," her confession would have been more effective, had she gone privately to each person she gossiped to, and humbly admitted her transgression, even calling it the sin that it was. And then, confessing to the pastor would have been in order.

A somewhat humorous illustration occurred in one church where a woman, feeling the guilt of a hypocritical life, stood during a church service and said, "If I've done anything wrong, to anybody, I want the church to forgive me."

A wise elderly gentleman in the congregation spoke up, "Tell us what you have done, Sister, so we *can* forgive you."

The Asbury College Confessions

An amazing movement of God occurred in 1970 on the campus of Asbury College in Wilmore, Kentucky. Perhaps the most phenomenal aspect of this 185-hour continuous chapel service was the students' confessions of their faults and sins. The results were restitution and restoration of relationships.

Prior to the unusual move of God in their midst, students at Asbury College had been meeting in small groups and fervently interceding in prayer for their classmates. They met once a week to share what the Lord was showing them in their personal devotions time. Some even stayed up all night to pray for others.

When chapel service began at Asbury College on that third day of February 1970, those attending from the small prayer groups anticipated a move of God. The faculty member who was to speak that day simply gave his testimony and described how he had been saved from sin as an adult. Then he invited students to come to the platform and tell what the Lord God had been showing them in their lives.

A holy hush filled the auditorium as students lined up to testify of their spiritual condition. Confessions of hypocritical lives began pouring from their mouths. They confessed shallow spiritual lives, then knelt at the altar to ask God to forgive them.

The revival extended even to the faculty. A professor of Bible humbled himself and confessed to being ill prepared to teach his classes.

The chapel service that was scheduled to last 50 minutes, lasted over a week—185 continuous hours! There was no disorderly conduct; no one spoke out of turn or fell to the floor in ecstasy. Humble confessing, praying, and praising became the order of the day.

When the revival began, the college president was out of town. Hearing about it in a phone call, he traveled home a few days after the revival began, sat in the back row, and just observed. One student came to him and confessed that she lied so much she didn't even realize she was doing it. He replied, "Can you remember the last person you lied to?"

"Yes," she said.

"Then go to that person, and confess your sin," he said. "Ask them to forgive you."

"That will kill me!" she said.

"No that will probably cure you," he replied.

As she did, the Lord brought to mind another person she had lied to, then another, then others. Three days later, she stood before the college president with glowing countenance and proclaimed, "I'm free! I just hit my thirty-fourth person and I'm free!"

Results of the students' honest confessions became phenomenal. Word quickly spread to secular colleges and news sources. At least 130 colleges (secular as well as religious) received traveling teams of eyewitness students who described the marvelous revival, spurred by prayer and confession. Asbury's president later observed that the less impressive the student representative seemed personally, the more God used him or her as a witness to others.

College president Dennis Kinlaw later described the revival. "It was honest, candid dealing with personal sin and with personal disobedience and with personal problems. Things that were simply traditions became living reality. There was an amazing openness and transparency."

Kinlaw also observed there was a proper restraint of the Holy Spirit in all the services, instead of an emphasis on gifts of the Spirit. Singing, the need for repentance, restitution, and repairing relationships became prominent. The student body sensed the need for bringing their lives into obedience to the highest and the best.

At the time of this writing, another phenomenal revival is taking place at Asbury University. It parallels the revival of 1970, characteristic with confession of sins, restitution, and pure worship of God. Although there is no one person in charge, all is orderly, peaceful and joyous.

Church members in our day of instant communication sometimes feel reluctant to confess faults and sins before the whole congregation. In the presence of notorious gossips who have not repented, that is understandable. In that case, if their sin hasn't affected the whole congregation, they could find a spiritual Christian to speak with, confess to, and pray with for cleansing. However, if their sin has divided the church or undermined those in authority, confessing to the entire congregation could serve as a deterrent for repeating the transgression.

The Nehemiah Principle

How did Nehemiah handle his discouraging situation? He paid attention to warnings from people in the know, those living outside Jerusalem. Some of the workers had neighbors on the opposing side. They warned the Jerusalem workers *ten times* of impending trouble.

After a brief respite, Nehemiah equipped his workers with weapons *in families*. In Nehemiah 4:14, we read his reminder to them of their obligations to their families, "Fight for your brethren, your sons, and your daughters, your wives, and your houses."

These people knew if they faltered in their tasks, not only would they suffer, but the ones they loved the most would suffer also. There is nothing like family ties to motivate people to action. Prayer keeps them on the right side.

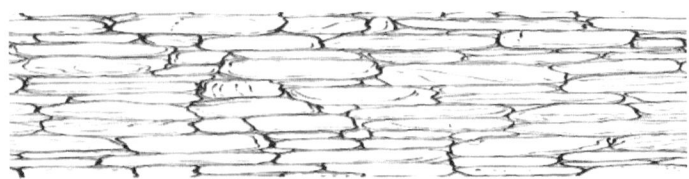

Dear Father in heaven, I feel like Nehemiah must have felt when threatened by destructive forces inside and out. The enemies on the inside are harder to spot then those on the outside.

Please give me wisdom to recognize those who may be used by the enemy of our souls to discourage and defeat. Some may not even realize they're doing it.

O Father, I know this is part of being a shepherd of men's souls. . I'm leaning heavily on You just now to lead and guide. In the name of Jesus, amen.

CHAPTER SIX

Drawn Swords—Help, Lord!

One young pastor learned a valuable lesson about taking time to pray through a difficult situation. Here are his words:

I was full of zeal and enthusiasm as I entered the ministry as an associate pastor. After the initial period of cooperation and camaraderie with the senior pastor, tensions came into our relationship. Regrettably, many in the congregation chose sides.

Fortunately, I had a good friend who was a neighboring pastor. Upon learning of the tensions in our church, he recommended the book *A Tale of Three Kings* by Gene Edwards. I read through it and wept under the weight of conviction. I realized that I was in grave danger of having a heart like unto Saul's rather than having a broken and contrite heart like David's.

Many years after having to work through the strained relationship with a fellow pastor, I was in an emergency meeting with several colleagues concerning an urgent matter that had the potential for a major division in a rather large ministry. Our boss had heard some things about me that were not true. He was convinced of his position and his words were strong and harsh.

He asked me to defend my position after I simply answered "no" to his question, "Are these things true?" I did not give any further explanation, nor did I strike back in any way. After more difficult conversation in the presence of my friends, I simply asked to be excused. Time went on and I told no one, not even my wife, about the encounter in the boardroom that day.

About a year later it was revealed who had actually said the divisive thing that I had been accused of saying. My boss came to me with a broken spirit and made a humble apology. He also apologized to the rest who were in the meeting that day.

An interesting footnote to this story took place about seven years after the incident. My boss used this story as an illustration in a sermon and once again took the humble approach. He admitted how wrong he had been and how badly he had hurt me.

A young lady who heard that message went to my wife and mentioned the incident to her. My wife had no idea what she was talking about. Why? Fortunately, I had told no one.

One of the lessons I learned was to be slow to speak, and "if someone throws a spear at you, verbal or otherwise, do not extract it from the wall behind you and throw it back."

Nehemiah was no stranger to threats. While serving as the king of Persia's cupbearer, his life potentially was in danger every day. It was no surprise to him, then, when onlookers tried to sabotage the work to which God called him.

What does that say to pastors today? If they really believe they are in spiritual warfare, they may be required to utilize out-of-the-ordinary measures to win conflicts, just as Nehemiah did.

Benefits of Spiritual Warfare

God blessed a small church in the Midwest with a young couple who recently emigrated from Africa. The husband of this family knew how to keep his faith strong through prayer and suggested a weekly prayer meeting for men. Those interested began meeting at 9:00 p.m. on Friday nights to pray and intercede for their congregation. Soon, they saw results. One elderly woman's grandson, who previously had no inclination toward spiritual matters, attended his first Sunday morning service. "I've never seen someone look so miserable," commented the pastor's wife at the dinner table after church.

Shortly afterward, his grandmother called the pastor to come and pray with her grandson late at night. The young adult man was sick of his sins, ready to forsake them and follow Christ. The men of the church had been praying, of course.

A middle-aged man, also not interested in God's ways, had indulged in deep sin. After being hospitalized he became troubled over his sinful ways, then sought and received God's forgiveness just before he died. He was the son-in-law of a regular member. The men had prayed for him during the Friday night prayer meeting.

Many people asked to be baptized during this time. Following the pattern in Acts 19:19–20, the church had a bonfire where spiritually revived people burned objects in their lives that held them bound to their former sins. The church enjoyed a period of exciting renewal while the men's prayer meeting existed.

※ ※ ※

As with any work which God blesses, opposition follows. Nehemiah and his workers faced threats to their lives. Workers from outlying areas forwarded intelligence that Sanballat and Tobiah were planning an attack. Some speculate that the Samaritans feared they would have to give back the land they acquired during the Babylonian captivity.

One pastor wrote, "Leadership takes much prayer, thinking, and planning. We will face challenges we never dreamed of, nor saw coming. Pastoring is more than showing up for a service. It is more than being on call, praying, and studying. Planning is crucial to success."

Fortunately, Nehemiah wasn't afraid of confrontations. With eyes solely on the glory of God and the cause of righteousness, and in the face of threats and taunts from his enemies, this wise leader set up a guard.

With great forethought, Nehemiah assigned each of the laborers to keep weapons nearby as they worked. Half the workers stood guard behind the builders and held spears, shields, bows, and armor. They strapped swords on their sides. Nehemiah even set up an alarm system; a man with a trumpet stayed by his side constantly, ready to sound a warning.

Curious onlookers probably thought this Jewish leader was overdoing the protection aspect. Nehemiah knew better. Some have speculated that he posted some of his armed guards behind the finished parts of the wall, out of sight to those approaching the city. Others may have been high on the wall, ready to drop large stones on anyone who posed a threat. They were serious about getting the job done.

As if that weren't enough, Nehemiah encouraged his out-of-town workers to spend the night in Jerusalem instead of returning home at the end of the day. There is strength in unity. These laborers operated in such a state of emergency that they even slept in their clothes.

Here are the words of a seasoned pastor with forty-five years of experience.

The Trowel and the Sword

We can be assured the devil is going to fight any believer who attempts to do anything for God. Nehemiah's enemies' goal was "to cause the work to cease."

This is my forty-fifth year of being in the pastorate, and to the best of my recollection the devil has made certain he has had a Sanballat and a Tobiah to stand in my path to hinder me each of those years. As long as the devil has breath, he will make sure there is a never-ending supply of Sanballats and Tobiahs to hinder the people of God.

Many young pastors graduate from Bible college, go out to pastor their first church, and think everyone is going to love them and be so appreciative they have come to town. But as soon as the honey leaves the honeymoon period, the modern-day Sanballats and Tobiahs are waiting with their swords drawn! And usually, not one professor at college took the time to teach them that these evil-hearted devils can be found in just about every church. Many young preachers are caught totally off guard. In many cases they are broken and sometimes beyond repair.

Nehemiah created a plan to defend their work as well as defend themselves from the evil deeds of Sanballat and Tobiah. Each person carried two items: first, a trowel and second, a sword. The trowel was used for working (building); the sword was used for fighting when the enemy attacked. If the enemy appeared suddenly, the builders would lay down the trowel and pick up a sword.

Our job is to win lost souls to the Lord Jesus Christ. The King of kings has given us orders to build for the Lord. Every soul won to the Lord is a stone added to the wall in the kingdom of God. But realize, once you start working for the King of kings, there will be modern-day Sanballats and Tobiahs ready to do everything they can to hinder the work. So, we must learn to fight back. But not to the point of neglecting our building.

When our church opened a Christian school several years ago, our state government mandated that we have a license to operate a preschool and after-school care program. We traveled to the state house and endured a lot of threatening.

Many young preachers would go through an experience like this and come out on the other side with lost perspective. They would expend so much energy fighting that, in the process, they would stop building their church. Pastors do the same with the abortion issue. I hate abortion with a passion. I despise our nation murdering over 65 million babies. However, if we are not careful, we can lose all perspective and drop everything to fight abortion all day, every day.

I support a couple of men to watch what the enemies of the Lord and of truth and the Bible are doing in my state legislature as well as on Capitol

Hill. While they watch what Sanballat and Tobiah are doing, I am running bus routes, training my members to win souls to Christ, and sending teenagers and adults out visiting every day of the week. My focus in on the gospel and the lost people in my community who are on their way to hell at breakneck speed.

However, when one of these sentries we support calls me to say, "Pastor, Sanballat and Tobiah are coming against your church or school"—or "They are bringing a group to fight over your First Amendment rights so you cannot preach against homosexuality," then I lay down my trowel, pick up a sword, and grab as many warriors as I can get, and then boldly go stand up to Sanballat and Tobiah. Most of the time, when you stand up to them, they will back down.

So, you may have to fight, and then once the battle is over, go back to the building project again. Don't let the devil get you off track by being enamored by the fight! Put your sword back into its sheath, pick up your trowel, and start laying stone to build the walls.

One last point: don't hang onto your sword too long. The longer you grasp it, the harder it is to put down.

Below is the story of a young couple that felt God leading them to start a Christian school, despite setbacks and discouragement. Their dilemma and determination resembled Nehemiah's.

One Pastor's Struggles and Success

Christian day schools were popping up all over our country in the 1980s. And no wonder! Godly parents were terribly concerned about their children's education. Bible reading and prayer were unlawful for our school-aged children. God had been rejected and expelled from our public school system and barred from the schoolyard.

Instead of the Ten Commandments hanging on the walls, policemen roamed the halls. Rapes and riots became commonplace. Drug use was rampant and high school pregnancies were a major problem. And so, concerned parents of America decided enough was enough. They had had it with all the immorality and academic nightmares.

Using the Bible as a strong foundation for every part of the curriculum, the *School of Tomorrow* was born. Even the smallest churches could use it.

I'm not sure the exact time when God began dealing with my heart about starting a school, but it grew until I knew we *had* to fight for our sons and daughters! The book of Nehemiah became very precious to my wife and me, almost like a blueprint to follow. Like Nehemiah, I recognized the need. There was a job to do. God's thumb was in my back. I was young and the task seemed huge. But my God was enough.

When I shared the burden of my heart with the church board members, they listened, but some did not share the same burden. Sometimes as leaders we must stand alone. Nehemiah stood alone as he wept and mourned and prayed over the ruins. And so did we, literally.

Praying over the Ruins

One afternoon I walked through the woods to a place where a foundation for a Christian day school had been laid years before. It, too, now lay in ruins. I knelt on some of the blocks of that old foundation and prayed, asking God to raise out of these stones a building that would bring glory and honor to His name.

Another day, another board meeting. One of the members addressed the others with a paraphrase from the Bible. "Brethren, if this is of God, then we would not want to fight against it. If it is of men, then it will come to naught."

And so, the board voted to start a Christian day school, only it would have to "float its own boat" (meaning the church wasn't going to support it financially in any way).

Wow! Now what? Where to go from here? I certainly didn't have the money to fund a school. Then I remembered a wealthy elderly aunt. I knew she had given money to a Bible school and college, so I wrote to her, explained the situation and asked if she would like to help in this endeavor.

The next morning when my wife came downstairs for her devotions, God was waiting and had something to say to her. She sensed He was grieved and sad. He seemed to say to her, "Why did you ask your aunt for money for the school? Why did you not ask Me?"

When I came down later, she shared all that God impressed on her heart. We knelt by the couch and asked God to forgive us and please help this aunt refuse. We made a covenant with God and each other that morning that we would do the work if He would pay the bills. One giant step forward.

We now saw how utterly dependent we were upon our God . . . exactly what God was aiming for!

The day came when my wealthy aunt sent a reply letter. My wife and I hugged each other, rejoiced, and sincerely praised the Lord; Aunt Merle had refused our request for money!
Okay, Lord, now it's all up to You!

Trusting in His promises and in the limitless resources of our Lord and Savior, we stepped out by faith and began to build.

The task, we knew, was way too big for us. Many times, we brought ourselves to the foot of the cross in utter discouragement, despair, and dismay. Then we heard our Father say, "Be not dismayed," and He would give us strength to continue.

We needed a school principal and God graciously provided one. Then he and his family needed a place to live. We searched the local newspaper and found a nice mobile home for sale, checked it out and said, "Let us pray about it."

One evening right at that time, we were taking the principal and his wife to a revival meeting about forty-five minutes away from our area. As we drove through the country, the principal noticed some nice, black Angus cows in a field. "We just need someone to donate about ten of those cows to the school and we could pay for the mobile home," he joked.

"Yeah!" we all laughed and agreed.

We went on to the revival meeting. After the service, a lady came to my wife and said, "We heard you're starting a school. I wanted to tell you that we've fattened ten cows and have already sent them to market. I'll be bringing the money to you when we get the check."

And we learned…God owns the cattle on a thousand hills.

What rejoicing all the way home! Soon the mobile home was signed for, sealed, and set up. All praises to Jesus!

The next hurdle came quickly; we faced a deadline. The principal and I had to travel to Texas to take the weeklong training for the school. I needed to purchase our airplane tickets. We'd need money for the motel room, our meals, and our fee to A.C.E. Altogether we needed about $2,000.

Our church was having revival services at that time. I had shared with the evangelist that we were trying to start a Christian day school. One night, as he and his wife got up to sing, he said, "God has put it on my heart to share something with you. Your pastor is trying to start a school and I know he needs some money. We're going to sing and while we do, I want you to be praying about what God would have you to do. If God doesn't say anything to you, don't feel you have to do anything. But, if He puts something on your heart, then obey God."

The evangelist and his wife sang. But before he could put down his accordion, a young man stood and said, "I have an old jeep I can sell for a thousand dollars. I'll give that money to the school."

The spirit of giving fell on the congregation and a large offering was given, more than enough to take care of the pressing need.

The next day, the enemy of our souls came in like a flood! He put great fear in some of those on our board. They were sure they would have to go to jail without bail —face lawsuits —live in orange suits! What if the school failed?

We Were at the Red Sea of Our Lives

How could we give back all the money people gave in that wonderful service just the night before? We didn't know who had given what. There was no way back … no way around … we *had* to go through. And so, I bought the plane tickets and packed our suitcases for Texas.

It seemed that with each victory, another battle had to be fought. This taught us three principles about stepping out and doing anything for God.

1. In order to win we would have to engage in spiritual warfare.
2. Every opportunity brings opposition.
3. We had to be vigilant to be victorious.

Sanballats and Tobiahs were all around us. Some from the community *laughed us to scorn.* They said, "There's another foundation. They'll get no further."

And God said, "Keep sweet! Do the work I've given you to do and leave them to me."

One day my wife shared with me that she had read Nehemiah 4:17–18 in her devotions that morning. "Everyone with one of his hands wrought in the work, and with the other hand held a weapon. For the builders, everyone had his sword girded by his side."

She prayed, "O God, what is the weapon we are to hold as we work?"

"The weapon of praise," God whispered to her heart. And so, we praised!

We started our school in the fall with twenty-eight students, and in a short while discovered there was a new lesson to learn. *If the devil can't discourage or defeat you from without, he'll try to come from within.*

Satan dealt us a terrible blow, both to the school and our church. Teachers said they weren't going to come back the next year. Students weren't going to come back. And we were in the process of building a new building!

One time stands out in my mind. We had gone to bed one night. Our bedroom windows faced east, the direction where our school was being built. I dropped off to sleep right away, but my wife could not get her eyes to close. She tossed and turned and sat up in bed. In the darkness she stared out the direction where the school was being built.

No teachers coming back! Of the students there's a lack! You just need to quit and pack! The enemy shouted in her ears. At that point she woke me up.

"Honey, why are we doing this?" she asked.

"Huh? What?" I stammered groggily. "Doing what, Shug?"

"Building! I mean teachers *and* students are saying they're not coming back. So, why are we doing this?"

"Because God said to!" My wife later said I barely managed to get the words out of my mouth before my eyes closed and I was snoring again.

"Oh! That's right...I had forgotten." Words formed in her mind, but never came to her lips, as there was no one to hear her anyway.

The fear of failure had been dealt with. We would obey God and leave all results with Him. If He wanted it to fail, it was okay! What a burden rolled off. Sweet peace came, along with needed sleep.

By the way, the teachers came back and there was even a small increase in students. Our building continued with God paying all the bills. Money came from all over the United States, sometimes from people we hadn't ever met.

And then, just as we were finishing our new building, getting ready to close for Christmas break, it was as though God slowed everything down. Ten dollars, twenty-five dollars, five dollars came in, whereas two thousand or five thousand had been coming in before that time. "Despise not the day of small things," God spoke to my heart, and so we praised Him for the small amounts. However, we needed about $5,000 to finish the plumbing and put down carpet, and it wasn't coming in!

"Borrow the money, Pastor! The bank will loan you the $5,000 and we can be in the new building for the second semester," some of our church members suggested. None wanted to be in more than we did, but I remembered our covenant with God.

"Lord," I prayed, "It would be like saying God started this, but He couldn't finish it!" No, we would wait, even if it meant *not* getting in our building until the next school year.

My wife's faith was sorely tried at this time, and we learned another lesson.

We had gone to our ministerial convention. We checked into our motel and shortly after, I left to attend a board meeting. As soon as I shut the door behind me, my wife knelt by a chair and began pouring her heart out to God.

"Lord," she prayed, "I'm so ashamed to tell You this, except I know You already know it. For the first time in my Christian life, it seems like I have no faith! And after all You have done for us, it makes me so ashamed. It feels like You've brought us all this way and now You've deserted us, forsaken us! Please help my faith, Father! Please pray for me, Jesus," she pleaded.

She reached for her devotional book and let it fall open. This is what the Scripture for the day said: "And the Lord said, 'Satan hath desired to have you, that he may sift you as wheat: but I have prayed for thee, that thy faith fail not'" (Luke 22:31–32).

The book continued, "Our faith is the center of the target at which God doth shoot when He tries us, and if any other grace shall escape untried, certainly faith shall not. There is no way of piercing faith to its very marrow like the sticking of the arrow of desertion into it. Faith must be tried, and *seemingly* desertion is the furnace, heated seven times, into which it must be thrust.[31]

All her doubts immediately disappeared, and faith *and* peace came again.

The Letter

A letter in our mailbox awaited us when we returned home from the ministerial convention. It bore the return address of the furnace company. The letter said there had been a problem with some of their furnaces having a cracked chamber, and in a few days, they would be sending someone to check ours at the school.

The furnace people came and found ours faulty. They replaced it with a new one and told us it was a good thing we had not moved into our building in January. Had we been using it, our building most likely would have burned to the ground. In my heart there was no doubt. As soon as the furnace was replaced, God sent in the needed money, and we completed the building.

When we dedicated it back to God, it was dedicated debt free!

God so wonderfully helped us. It wasn't long until the board members who were in doubt about the school saw the hand of God at work in it all. The day came when they unanimously voted to make the school an extension of the church and began to support it.

The Nehemiah Principle

Closing words from the authors of the above account: Nehemiah's example reveals to us that every real work for God must begin with ourselves, and how we are to face opposition from without and discouragement from within.

We learned that the circumstances we could have resented, people and situations we may have found desperately difficult, had been the very means of conforming us into the image of the Lord Jesus and making Him so dear and precious to us. Remember, the God of Nehemiah is our God, too.

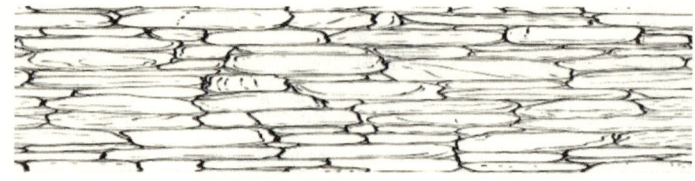

Dear Lord, sometimes it's hard to see what You are doing when I'm up to my eyeballs in difficulties. This leader needs help! Please give me faith to believe in the cause of righteousness You have called me to, wisdom like Nehemiah, to work like it all depends on me, and faith to pray like it all depends on You. In Christ's name, amen.

CHAPTER SEVEN

Reforming Bad Behavior

Pastor Nate had a unique problem. Arriving as the pastor of a sizeable church, he discovered the worship leader lived a hypocritical life. Neighbors described the man's fits of anger, which they could hear from up the road as he shouted at his family. His lifestyle was inconsistent with the claims of the gospel. Removing the man from his position could have been problematic, since he had ties to the most strategic members on the board.

What does a pastor do when the most influential person in his church is a descendant of its local founders, yet not spiritually qualified for his position? More about that later in this chapter.

Conflict Resolution 101

First, let's see what Nehemiah faced at this juncture of his leadership challenges. After Nehemiah moved to protect the people of Jerusalem from enemies *outside* the walls, his next step was to keep them from destroying one another *inside* the walls. The problem was the rich people in Jerusalem who took advantage of their poorer brothers and sisters in the area.

A little history: Those who returned to rebuild Jerusalem's walls recently had been exiles in Persia. They were virtually penniless upon arrival in Jerusalem. In addition, a famine forced the new immigrants to borrow money to feed their families.

Taking advantage of the immigrants' misfortune, wealthy people in the city loaned them money at high interest rates. God gave his people strict orders *not* to do this in Exodus 22:25 and Deuteronomy 23:19-20.

One misfortune led to another. The poorer people, already in debt, had to mortgage their land, vineyards, and houses not only to repay the loans, but also to pay taxes to the Persian monarch. In one last act of desperation, these destitute citizens gave their children as slaves to pay debts to their wealthy national relatives.

When Nehemiah heard the outcry of his people, he became very angry. Nehemiah 5:7 tells us the man of God didn't immediately call a board meeting. Instead, he said, "I consulted with myself" (Nehemiah 5:7). What was he doing while working through his anger? He was analyzing the situation before reacting.

In some religious circles there is a belief that any type of anger is wrong. A wise teacher at a Bible college addressed this issue, giving a balanced view to sincere students seeking answers.

This teacher reminded his class there is a time for *righteous indignation* (and no, that's not another name for a temper tantrum). *Righteous anger comes when a person sees God's reputation or another person being violated.* His own rights have nothing to do with it.

For example, if a Christian walked down the street and saw a gang of teenage boys assaulting a helpless woman, it would be right to react angrily and try to stop them.

Or if a pastor walked into an empty church building and saw a group of rowdies ripping up hymnals and Bibles, it definitely would be a time for anger and strong confrontation.

Notice, however, when Nehemiah *himself* was criticized by naysayers, he didn't retaliate in anger. That, my friend, is the difference between righteous anger and carnal anger.

After taking time to ponder his next step (in the spirit of the New Testament Matthew 18), Nehemiah privately went to the guilty and told them their sin. Then he called an assembly.

You can read the account of this godly leader's solution in the book of Nehemiah chapter five. If it's been a while since you've read it, a quick review of Nehemiah's solution to this problem will be helpful.

God's man for the job knew the problem and he knew the answer. First, he reminded his guilty Jewish brothers that he led by example. He spent twelve years as governor of Jerusalem without taking a salary. He fed 150 people every day at his own expense.

By living an example before his followers, Nehemiah had a right to take his brothers to task for their bad behavior. When he laid out the problem before the guilty, they became speechless. It was impossible to deny the obvious.

This wise leader then took bold action. He commanded the wealthier men of the city to restore the lands, vineyards, olive yards and houses—and a hundredth part of the money as well as the food they had extracted from their fellow Jewish brothers.

Nehemiah's next action probably puzzles those in our day, unfamiliar with ancient practices. He "shook his lap" and wished a curse upon those who failed to carry out their promise to restore the unjust payment from their countrymen.

By that act he wished for those who failed to comply to be scattered abroad out of their own lands, just as he scattered the folds of his garment. To be "scattered" from family and friends was about the worst thing that could happen in the culture of his day.

Notice, the citizens willingly complied when their leader presented the facts clearly. Nehemiah. 5:13 says, "And all the congregation said, Amen, and praised the LORD. And the people did according to this promise."

Sometimes it takes someone from the outside to see clearly what has been under our noses all the while. And it takes bold action to face down bold sin.

Pastor Charles faced a situation that plagues many churches: jealousy over the piano and organ bench. After much prayer, he addressed it with bold action. Here is the story in his own words.

Confrontations on the Organ Bench

The biggest hindrance I faced in one of my pastorates was a quarrel over who played the church organ. To make matters worse, it began the very first week I arrived, and I didn't even know about it until it became almost too late.

In many churches, there appears a lack of people who either can, or are willing, to play the piano or organ. However, this church was blessed with a lot of musical talent. And, as I soon found out, there was someone who did not like playing second fiddle!

To be clear, there should have been no quarrel. The church body voted on a church musician each year (who typically played the piano), and it was common practice for the elected musician to choose their accompanist. However, the current elected church musician also was an accomplished organ player. So, her practice was to play the organ and then choose someone to play along on the piano.

Over the course of the year there would be some variation whenever certain people would be absent. During some of those times, the elected musician would play the piano instead and there was again a large group of people who could play the organ.

At some point a previous organist was asked to play for several services, which she did. Then, when she was not able to attend a service, she tried to keep control of the organ bench by asking someone else to play in her absence. This started a conflict with the elected musician who actually had this responsibility, a conflict that seemed to persist during the entire time of my ministry there.

The week I arrived, the elected musician's husband (who also was a board member) decided not to bother the new pastor with the budding conflict. Instead, he took advantage of a church gathering to tell the prior organist in no uncertain terms that she was not in charge. Unfortunately, his lack of tact only served to exacerbate the problem. By the time the situation came to my attention, battle lines were drawn, and sides taken.

I went to see those on both sides. The elected musician was distraught and ready to resign. I told her to stay the course. She was not in the wrong, as the church election did not stipulate that she had to play the piano. It was her call as to whom she chose to accompany her. I did have words for her husband, though. I felt if he had gotten me involved from the beginning, I could have salvaged the situation. Now, he had pushed the crisis beyond repair.

The second person I visited thought the elected musician should play the piano and not monopolize the organ. She would not accept the church board's statement that it was the elected one's right to do so. I didn't get far with my counsel. There wasn't anything to be done as long as the church membership had voted things as they were.

The hindrances kept rolling in. A whispering campaign started. I believe a nonmember who asked to join the church lied to me in the interview process because he sided with the previous organist and wanted to try to vote her in as church musician.

Confusion reigned with some of the older saints who didn't know what was happening. But the straw that broke the camel's back was when I heard there were people in town who had nothing to do with our church, asking what in the world was going on in our congregation. I knew then that someone had been talking about the situation publicly.

As I had already had private conversations with each side—and it had not worked—I decided to address the matter in church. If people were going to speak out publicly, then I could too.

One Sunday evening I shut down the livestream and explained the whole situation to the congregation. When I got to the part that it was affecting our influence in the town, I made it very clear that this was unacceptable. I said I understood how both sides felt. However, the church's ability to be a witness in our own town was far more important than our feelings in a matter that was very petty at the end of the day. I declared it was time to bury the hatchet (and not in each other's heads), and that if I ever heard rumblings about the situation again, I would take even more drastic action than just talking about it.

Thankfully, the church at large was able to move on. Unfortunately, some individuals never really could move on and were damaged until their death. I learned then, and it has been reinforced many times since, that problems not dealt with the right way, often have a way of snowballing into major hindrances for the church. But, the work of the church is worth fighting for, even if it requires standing up against the offending church members among us.

Bold Sin, Bold Action

Back to Pastor Nate. What does a pastor do when the most influential man in his church is a descendant of the family who donated land for church use—but he is not qualified to lead? To complicate matters, this man also was related to sympathetic board members.

After much deliberation and "consulting with himself," the young minister stopped calling this worship leader to the platform, and instead chose others in his place. It was a bold move. No one had dared deny leadership positions to this powerful, wealthy family.

One day the man, now humiliated because of his step down from leadership, confronted the pastor in the church parking lot.

"Why don't you just leave," he told Pastor Nate. And then he reminded the pastor, "We were here long before you came, and we'll be here long after you're gone."

Of course, those unkind words stuck like a dagger in the heart of the man of God. But he knew he had done the right thing. Fortunately, the story did not end there. As it turned out, "Wisdom is justified of her children" (Matthew 11:19b).

When the influential family left and took nearly half the congregation with them, the remaining members panicked. Many were elderly and lived on fixed incomes. How would they keep the church going with limited funds?

God provided in a miraculous way by turning tragedy into triumph. It happened like this:

The church hired a crew to replace the roof on their large building. The day the carpenters' crew tore off the old roof, a heavy rainstorm appeared suddenly. Before they could tack down enough tarps, heavy rainfall soaked through the exposed parts of the roof. Moisture dripped through the roof, the ceiling, and into the sanctuary. Overhead lights resembled fishbowls filled with water.

What appeared to be a disaster resulted in a blessing. The church's insurance company paid for the damage. This former struggling congregation received enough money to replace the water-soaked ceiling, the songbook racks, and even the carpet.

The disgruntled family moved to another church, where they quickly moved into leadership positions. After their exodus, Pastor Nate's church experienced growth and spiritual prosperity. Several newly saved young people began attending, and their presence sparked enthusiasm among those who remained. While it's not always easy to do the right thing—and we don't always see results—it's always right.

The Nehemiah Principle

One of the difficult tasks a pastor faces is standing at the gateway of his church, protecting his people from those who would harm the flock. Sometimes it means going toe-to-toe with those much older, who have been "in the way" for a long time. The wise minister will saturate himself with prayer, asking God for wisdom to be respectful of those who are older, yet firm in his stand for the right.

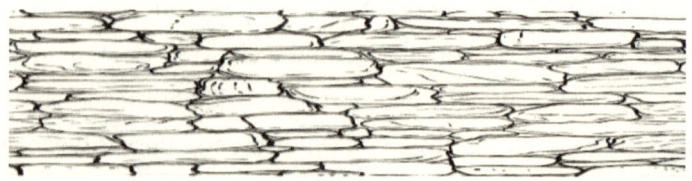

Dear Heavenly Father, traditions sometimes help and sometimes hinder. Please give us godly people in leadership positions as well as in the pews. The world is watching to see how well we interact with each other. I pray You will grant me boldness when needed, and Christ-like love when it's necessary to use bold action. In the name of the One who overthrew tables in the Temple area, yet wept over Jerusalem, amen.

CHAPTER EIGHT

Fatigue and Frustration: Friends of Your Enemies

Pastor Phil came home exhausted after a full day of visiting hospital patients. He had counseled a troubled family and carried burdens for others in his congregation. The weary minister kissed his wife and sighed. "I feel like the little Dutch boy with his finger in the dike. Every time I plug a leak, a new one pops out."

Fatigue and burnout can happen to anyone involved in intense spiritual warfare or demanding mental and physical labor. Our minds and bodies are meant for regular rest and renewal. That is not always possible, however, when emergency situations present themselves. Nehemiah's workers constantly looked over their shoulders, anticipating danger—a formula for discouragement.

Many pastors can attest that in some projects, the halfway point becomes a time of fatigue. It happened to those under Nehemiah's leadership. We read about it in Nehemiah 4:10. "And Judah said, The strength of the bearers of burdens is decayed, and there is much rubbish; so that we are not able to build the wall."

Let's see what happened to a pastor who wanted to start an outreach ministry. The story below, in his own words, illustrates the benefits of staying at the job.

Shouldn't We Try Another Street?

Bus ministry has always been an area that I feel churches should try to incorporate into their outreach. I was a product of a bus ministry.

I attended a few conventions, trying to get the proper tools. I took the handouts and found creative ways to use route sheets for visitation.

To begin, my wife and I prayed about where to start inviting children and parents to Sunday school. You may say, "That's easy; wherever you see a child, you stop and invite." Instead, we felt we needed God's direction where to start our outreach ministry.

After a time, we felt Chestnut Street was the place the Lord was leading us to start our house-to-house campaign. We planned to meet at the church on Saturdays at 1:00 p.m. and quit at 3:00 p.m.

We soon found out there were a lot of houses where no one wanted to answer the door.

Our group developed a worksheet where we wrote down each address, the name of the parents and each of the children, a phone number, and whether they already attended a church. (This was in the day when people didn't mind giving out information.) I would collect the notebooks from those who joined us on these visitations and then type the information into the handouts for the next week.

We began with addresses already on the worksheets, hoping to find someone home where we didn't have any information, and swing by those houses with children, to see if they had decided to come to Sunday school that week.

One of our faithful helpers found this a trial to his patience. We had covered only two or three blocks after working the same street for a little less than a month. He came to me with a serious tone and said, "Pastor, don't you think we ought to try another street?" I told him we could, but we needed to finish this one first. Would you believe, we never did finish Chestnut Street? Here's why.

One of the mothers who was nice enough to talk to us a few weeks, finally consented to allow her seven-year-old daughter to come to Sunday school. So, we picked up our first little Sunday school scholar in our own van. We were so excited and yet unsure how we were going to make a bus outreach work.

The next Saturday visitation started as usual, with our group going to each house and getting new information, and then stopping at the house with our only bus child. The mother told us how much her daughter loved her Sunday school teacher, and she couldn't wait for Sunday school again. Then she asked us if we had asked her neighbor about their children going to Sunday school. We told her we did, but they already went to another church. She looked at me strangely when I told her that. She walked off her porch and said over her shoulder, "Follow me."

I stood and watched the mother of our first bus child talk her neighbor into letting their children come to Sunday school with her daughter. Then that family got a friend on the corner to come. Another Saturday we stopped in when a mother across town was visiting, and she wanted her children to be picked up. Each week we had a new family to pick up, surprisingly, from down Chestnut Street. And yes, they told us they already went to church. Somehow, I had trouble believing that.

Although the pastor above had a happy ending, life doesn't always go that way. At times, pastoring can feel like living in the emergency room at the hospital. Each person's situation can appear to them as an emergency. Parishioners hope the pastor can magically produce a solution to their problem—right away, if possible. Often, he wishes he could. Those who have raced to the hospital to console parents of a dying child know the feeling of helplessness it produces.

Out of necessity, ministers of small congregations wear many hats. This description aptly fit Pastor Jerry. Unwittingly, he trained his small flock to depend on him for nearly everything. If an elderly widow failed to get her car started, she called Pastor Jerry to come fix it. Did the church furnace malfunction? The elders knew Jerry could be counted on to tinker with it. Brother Leroy needed a haircut. He came by the parsonage on Pastor Jerry's day off to ask for a free one.

This minister of many talents gladly helped his flock with their needs. However, he learned by painful experience what happens when the leader fails to delegate authority to others under his guidance. First, it deprives others of exercising their talents for God's glory. Second, he experiences fatigue and burnout.

One incident became the proverbial straw that broke the camel's back. Harry, a middle-aged man, called an already-exhausted Pastor Jerry out of his warm bed on a cold night to see why his car wouldn't start.

Finding the vehicle parked along the street in a crime-ridden big city, Jerry lifted the car's hood and peered inside while cautiously glancing over his shoulder. He then crawled under the car to check for a possible leak in the gas tank. No problem there. The problem was Harry. He forgot to notice his gas gauge registered empty.

After years of tirelessly trying to be all things to his flock, Jerry showed telltale signs of burnout. His extroverted personality transformed into one of quiet withdrawal. He avoided speaking on the phone. Instead of spending time visiting parishioners or studying for sermons, Jerry lay on the sofa with his face turned toward the wall.

The wife of this weary minister knew it was time to seek help. She contacted the group Ministering to Ministers and reserved a spot at their next seminar. After spending several days with professional counselors and other pastors, this exhausted couple realized they had to take a break to heal their bodies, minds, and spirits. That led to Jerry's and his wife's painful decision to resign their pastorate.

Ministering to Ministers got the couple started on a journey of healing, which took a very long time (though not all take as long).[32] These ministerial servants now know they must set boundaries if they want to maintain healthy bodies, minds, and spirits.

Famous leadership mentor John C. Maxwell has said, "All true leaders have learned to say no to the good in order to say yes to the best."

The John Wesley Syndrome

Those who read John Wesley's journals often come away with the idea that the leader of the Methodist movement kept a grueling schedule 365 days a year. We read that he stood at the mouth of coal mines at 4:30 a.m. and preached to workers before they entered the mines. He tells of preaching four times a day and writing books while traveling on horseback to his next meeting.

Wesley's exhausting schedule could make today's minister blush in embarrassment. Preaching at 4:30 a.m. after having personal devotions seems daunting, at the least. We need to realize, however, that those were the *highlights* of this great man's schedule; they didn't happen every day. Wesley wrote those accounts of his experiences to spur his ministers to selfless serving.

Wesley's personal diary lends a refreshing perspective. Like many others in his era, Wesley wrote the account of his everyday life in code. Fortunately, Dr. Richard Heitzenrater of the Perkins School of Theology managed to decipher Wesley's complex code. Through it we see that Wesley didn't set endurance records every single day. He *did* take time to rest.[33]

Jesus reminded his followers in Matthew 11:30, "For my yoke is easy, and my burden is light." Most of us think of a yoke as a wooden frame connecting oxen or other large animals when they plow a field.

However, the *GNU Collaborative International Dictionary of English*, tells us a yoke can be "*as much land as may be plowed by a pair of oxen in a day.*" (Thank you to our pastor for mentioning this.) Jesus may have been telling his followers they didn't have to cram twenty hours of work into a twenty-four-hour time period.

Nehemiah had the answer to fatigue and failure; he wisely delegated tasks. His workers on the wall became discouraged at hauling away so much debris from the building site. Then, when they heard the enemies' plans to disrupt the work, they were ready to quit. Nehemiah wouldn't allow them to do that.

"And I looked, and rose up, and said unto the nobles, and to the rest of the people, Be not afraid of them: remember the LORD, which is great and terrible (majestic) and fight for your brethren, your sons, and your daughters, your wives, and your houses" (Nehemiah 4:14).

The first step in maintaining momentum in a good work is for the leader to keep the vision in front of his flock. We're all human and prone to forget our initial enthusiasm for a project when things get tough.

Nehemiah also reminded his workers to fight for their families. An instructor in a natural childbirth class motivated her students with this illustration: "When you are in labor to have a baby and feel like you don't have enough strength to give birth, it's like climbing a mountain and thinking you can't go another step. Then you look back and see a bear coming after you. Suddenly you get energy you didn't know you had."

While that may be a humorous example, it applies to both the rebuilding of the wall and spiritually contending for our families. What better motivation than imagining your loved ones enjoying peace and safety because of your effort. And what better "bear" behind you than the thought of your children and grandchildren being attacked if you let up your effort.

During ancient warfare, clans or tribes employed a standard-bearer. This man held the flag that represented his tribe while soldiers clashed arms for ownership of land. For instance, the tribe of Judah may have used a drawing of a lion. When the battle became hottest, the standard-bearer raised the flag high to remind his fellow soldiers of their families at home. So must the pastor become the standard-bearer of his flock, keeping before his people the responsibilities God has entrusted to them for those they know and love.

The Nehemiah Principle

Pastor Jerry could have avoided burnout if he had followed Nehemiah's example. Although a minister may be a man of many skills, his main task is to see that others are trained to meet menial needs of his flock, thus freeing him for study, prayer, and visitation.

One of the greatest favors a pastor can give his church is seeing that the members develop their gifts. In one congregation, Helen was painfully shy, yet blossomed surprisingly when given the opportunity to teach children's church. The woman who blushed and stammered when speaking to adults became a dynamic teacher of children.

Likewise, Mike, not a natural leader, enjoyed helping his congregation by landscaping the church grounds. Carol loved to clean, and used her gift of organization to keep the sanctuary and restrooms sparkling. Another church designated one Saturday a month for mechanics in their congregation to do minor repairs on vehicles belonging to widows and needy families. All in the church can find ways to use their gifts, whether great or small. The pastor's job is to see that it happens.

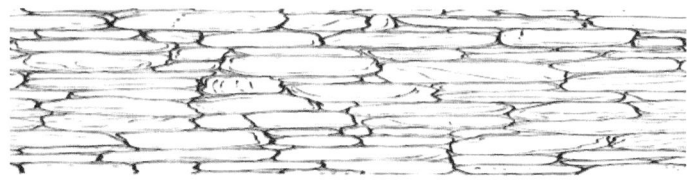

Dear Heavenly Father, I'm not tired of the battle as much as I'm tired in the battle. Please show me how to delegate tasks to others. I ask for wisdom and discretion as I lead others to find their place of ministry in our flock. In the name of Christ our Lord, amen.

CHAPTER NINE

Naysayers and Game Players

Pastor Steve experienced an example of distraction to his ministry. His denomination became polarized over an issue when leaders voted to take action that some considered unbiblical. Good men stood on both sides of the debate. Some pastors disagreed so strongly with their leaders' decision that they resigned their churches.

Steve felt tugged in both directions. He admired men on both sides; what should he do? We will consider his difficult decision later in this chapter.

In Nehemiah's time, the Jerusalem wall-building project was nearly finished when conflict reared its ugly head. We shouldn't be too surprised when this happens. Satan uses intimidation in many forms to hinder God's work.

The only remaining part of the construction project was setting the doors on the city gates. Once that happened, Jerusalem's citizens could feel a greater sense of security, and then they could concentrate on rebuilding worship practices and regaining their crumbling culture.

Of course, enemies of the Jewish people became frantic to stop the progress. If they couldn't intimidate the workers, they could attack their leader.

Their first tactic called for *distracting* Nehemiah from his main task. Four times these hecklers called for a meeting with him. Four times he refused. Let's look at these strategies because Satan's tactics haven't changed much over the centuries.

As mentioned in chapter four, distracting a leader can take the form of pretended friendship—offering to include him in the Good Ol' Boy Club. "Come and meet with us in the plain of Ono," these distractors cordially invited (Nehemiah 6:2). In today's vernacular they would have said, "Let's hang out together."

The Diversion Version

This chapter began by describing Pastor Steve's modern-day dilemma similar to Nehemiah's. Steve's denomination experienced a sharp division over a controversial issue. He knew that lending his support to either side would influence many good people.

While Steve prayed about this critical decision, a denominational leader phoned him. "The main board met and wants to extend to you a position on a certain board," he said. This position offered a unique chance to influence those in his denomination.

"Well, could I pray about it before I give you an answer?" Steve asked.

"Of course. Just let us know your decision."

After hanging up the phone, this puzzled pastor and wife debated the pros and cons of his choice. Tilting her head to one side, Mrs. Steve said, "You know what? If you accept this position, it will imply that you endorse what we feel is the denomination's wrong stand on that hot issue everyone's talking about right now."

Steve knew his church was in a pivotal position. His membership included those who could contribute large sums of money to his denomination. Whatever decision he led his church to make probably would sway others who were waffling about the issue.

"I think you're right," he replied. "I'll call the board member and tell him I can't accept the offer." He placed the call and felt relieved.

A few weeks later, the important official called again, repeating the same tempting offer. Steve knew that being a member of this board could open doors for any young pastor. It also could lead to being included in a denominational clique.

"Thanks for the kind offer, but I really don't feel I can accept," Steve replied for the second time. Though never included in a high-profile denominational clique, Steve's mind and heart remained free of condemnation. Following Nehemiah's example, he refused to join the ones feigning friendship as a means of using his influence.

The Invitation

The passage from Nehemiah 6:2 sheds light on Sanballat's and Geshem's motives. They sent a messenger to God's chosen leader, feigning concern for his welfare. I like to imagine Nehemiah bent over, inspecting the wall when the messenger arrived. He probably stopped, dusted his hands on his side, and mopped the sweat from his brow. Then he drew himself to his full height and listened to the messenger sent by his enemies.

I like to think Nehemiah barely looked at the man before abruptly turning away and saying over his shoulder, "Tell Sanballat and Tobiah I am doing a great work, so that I cannot come down. Why should the work cease whilst I leave it and come down to you?"

The plain of Ono, where Nehemiah's enemies had invited him to come, was about twenty miles north of Jerusalem. God gave this leader wisdom to know that if he deserted his post, his enemies could enter his domain and wreak havoc among the residents under his care.

Enemies Within and Without

Another way the enemy of our souls attacks a good work is through *disunity*. Below is an account written by a pastor who experienced enemies hidden within his work.

Many times, I have thought about the way Nehemiah conducted himself. He had to be prepared always for attack by the opposition. Extra precautions even slowed the speed of the work.

In Nehemiah 6:12 we read, "And lo, I perceived that God had not sent him." Nehemiah realized that not all opposition was in the open. My experiences earlier in my ministry caused me to face a situation that would have put me in Nehemiah's shoes.

A person attending our church began to visit our new contacts. This became a problem when the people they had visited then felt uncomfortable coming to our church. I backed away from the situation and committed the troublemaker to God, not wanting to create a bigger problem. As a congregation, we prayed that God would resolve this huge issue.

During this time, there was a constant undertow of uneasy feeling in the flock. I perceived a problem but was unsure of its source.

For most of my ministry, I was self-supporting. This added to the stress, of course. I had to drive lonely stretches of road where we lived, yet it also gave me many hours to spend time with God.

One day as I was driving and crying, the Lord started speaking to me. I had a hat in my truck and felt the Lord impressing me with the thought, *Turn the hat upside down. When you are done crying over a problem, put it in the hat.* Yes, these problems were some of the first in the hat. When I finished unloading the problems, the Lord impressed on me again, *Now, dump them in the trash can! They are no longer your problems; they are mine. Leave them alone!*

The problems remained for a while, but eventually the individual causing the open opposition left. This helped significantly when working with new contacts. Yet, we still had a constant uneasy feeling and undertow that perplexed me.

Someone approached me later and said they could no longer be part of our church, and they left without further notice. We wondered how we were going to operate without them. The amazing part was, instantly the undertow was gone! The same amount of work now is being done with fewer people.

When Nehemiah's enemies discovered their first four invitations were rebuffed, they then combined false accusations with one of the most difficult threats for a leader to handle: *insinuation*. Some choose to call it passive-aggressive behavior.

Sanballat was a master of passive-aggressive behavior: quiet insults. After four unsuccessful attempts to divert Nehemiah, he sent an open letter.

In ancient times, important letters to governors were carefully rolled or folded, then sealed and delivered in silk bags tied with colorful ribbons. Sending an open letter that anyone could read was a non-verbal slap in the face. It implied that the governor didn't deserve respect. And Nehemiah, accustomed to Persian court affairs, would have noticed this.[34] The open letter also could have served as an alert to those looking for reasons to remove Nehemiah from his leadership role.

The content of Sanballat's letter was accusatory. In today's vernacular it might have read, "You are accused of treason against the king of Persia. In fact, it's going to be reported to him. It is common knowledge that you are setting yourself up to be king of Judah. Come, let's discuss this matter before it gets out of hand."

Sanballat, of course, was hinting, "Come justify yourself before us." This enemy knew that while Nehemiah was absent, Sanballat's cronies could slip in and wreck a good work.

Nehemiah knew when to ignore insinuation. He was a picture of wisdom in shoe leather...er, sandals. I like to think he barely looked up at the messenger before turning back to his work. "Tell Sanballat and Tobiah it's a figment of their imagination. There is no such thing done" (Nehemiah 6:8).

Satan's work through Sanballat and Tobiah received a temporary setback, yet they weren't finished. Seeing their fifth effort refused, they appealed to what they imagined might have been Nehemiah's possible weak point: *fear*.

When Fear Becomes Sin

Shemaiah, the mercenary false prophet, urged Nehemiah to think of his own safety. "Let's hide in the temple and shut the doors, lest someone try to kill you while you sleep," he urged. *A godly minister once warned, "Be careful of the man who has heard from God about your business since you have."*

What would have happened if Nehemiah had gone along with the false prophet's plan? First, it would have made him appear a coward and a weak leader. He would have disobeyed the protocol that allowed only priests in the temple area. Most importantly, it would have enabled Jerusalem's enemies to creep in and overtake the city. In addition, Sanballat could have declared an end to Nehemiah's rule and possibly taken over as governor of Jerusalem. (Pastors sometimes must contend with those who envy their positions and organize a coup to implement it. But that's a story for another day.)

When tempted to save our own necks, it is wise to recall a saying our Bible college president used in chapel services. "It's never right to do wrong in order to get a chance to do right."

The Nehemiah Principle

Commentator Matthew Henry said, "If our enemies cannot frighten us from duty, or deceive us into sin, they cannot hurt us."[35] So, pastor, it appears that standing against opposition requires two components: prayer and watchfulness.

Matthew Henry also observed, "If we think to secure ourselves by prayer, without watchfulness, we are slothful, and tempt God; if by watchfulness, without prayer, we are proud, and slight God. Either way, we forfeit his protection."

Charles Spurgeon said, "No oppressor can rage against us unless the Lord permits; why then do we fear? He who gives our foe permission to annoy us in measure, holds the other end of his chain and will keep him within bounds. In holy confidence let us stand still and see the salvation of God."[36]

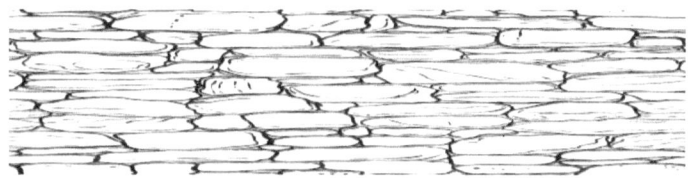

Dear Heavenly Father, The enemy of my soul has been in his business for a long time. I am, by contrast, inexperienced. Please give me sanctified wisdom and discretion to recognize enemies in sheep's clothing. In the name of your Son, the wisest shepherd who ever breathed earth's air, amen.

CHAPTER TEN

Prickly Problems and Proper Protocol

Pastor Phil and Greg, his Sunday school superintendent, made a winning team. Phil was the Energizer bunny; Greg was the tortoise. Phil motivated Greg to rise from his chair and become more physically active. Greg influenced Phil to become more disciplined in his everyday life.

Phil grew up around outwardly respectable people who thought good works merited a passport to heaven. His gift was reaching religiously smug souls. Greg, by contrast, connected with those who tasted the dregs of deep sin and knew they needed help. God used Greg's former alcoholism to reach those whom Pastor Phil struggled to help. The ministry of these two men dovetailed as each used their gifts to bring souls to the kingdom of God.

Another winning combination appeared with Nehemiah and his friend, Ezra. God placed the efficient scribe at Nehemiah's elbow for a reason. Ezra had a stellar reputation for wisdom, godliness, and a zeal for seeing God's work done properly. His scholarly, solid counsel was a perfect balance for Nehemiah's active, yet sometimes hot, zealous nature. We'll read more about Nehemiah's zeal and the hair-pulling incident in chapter twelve of this book.

Ezra's genealogy could be traced all the way back to Aaron, Moses' brother. Some scholars think that Ezra collected the scattered versions of the Law of Moses and compiled them together again to benefit the Jewish people suffering from ignorance of God's ways during the Babylonian captivity. This man, chosen to aid Nehemiah at a crucial time, proved trustworthy. In fact, he was so scrupulous that the king of Persia previously allowed him to return to Jerusalem with the gold and silver vessels that were stolen when Jerusalem's enemies ransacked the city.

In addition to being trustworthy, Ezra proved wise in realizing the depths of mankind's depravity. He knew that when his group traveled, marauders would roam the desert, robbing and plundering. Thus, he did what any God-fearing man would do: proclaimed a fast to pray for his group's protection (Ezra 8:21).

When we realize Ezra's journey took at least four months and covered several hundred miles, it seems logical that he kept a sharp watch over his entourage. As he arrived with the temple treasures, Ezra arranged for the gold and silver to be weighed to make sure it all was there. (Ezra 8:33-34).

Looking for a Few Good Men

Anyone who has guided a project to completion will tell you the job isn't over when carpenters pound the last nail, or mortar the last stone in place. Original purposes sometimes are forgotten in the busyness of daily life. And so, Nehemiah instituted an orderly plan for maintaining his beloved city.

The wall was finished and the gates hung in a record fifty-two days. To prevent a repeat performance of their national disobedience, Nehemiah and Ezra knew they must establish leadership roles and rules. They needed two wise, godly men to lead the newly organized city.

Filling an order for leadership positions can be challenging. Those in leadership must be dead to personal gain, must not oppress the people they lead, and refuse to take bribes or abuse their authority. Nehemiah found two. Hanani, Nehemiah's brother was appointed to be the new governor. This brother was the one who alerted Nehemiah to the state of affairs in Jerusalem in the first place. Hananiah, overseer of the king's palace, became Hanani's right-hand man. Both men had reputations for honesty, faithfulness, and respect for their God. They knew how to anticipate future circumstances and prepare for them. Nehemiah recognized that those who manage just the present circumstances become only managers, not leaders with an eye for the future.[37] Although

Nehemiah didn't seem interested in gaining a reputation or a legacy for himself, it seems obvious he chose leaders who would further a legacy for God.

While still acting as governor, Nehemiah knew the newly established residents of Jerusalem still carried heathen ideas and practices from their years of captivity. It would take time to reprogram their thinking. Thus, he wisely laid down a few rules for the entire city to follow.

First, the gates of Jerusalem must be kept locked until the sun grew hot. This assured that the residents would be awake and able to respond to sudden attacks. Then, because the city was large and the buildings few, the residents needed enough families living there to furnish a guard.

At first this caused a problem. Many people now were settled on established farms and homes in the suburbs. After the Assyrians demolished Jerusalem several decades previously, the remaining families fled to outlying areas of Judea to escape further exploitation. Nehemiah had to choose a way to persuade his national brethren to move back to Jerusalem and settle within the walls. There could be no accusations of partiality, no room for complaints in the final decision.

Nehemiah's answer reflected thoughtful consideration. He started by settling those who had returned from the Babylonian captivity first. The idea was to place them in the cities possessed by their ancestors under the original direction of Joshua.

Then another dilemma appeared. Some ancestries couldn't be traced. A helicopter view of the Jewish nation is helpful at this point. The people of the northern kingdom had been conquered and carried away first. They could never again be fully traced as a separate people. The Assyrians had deported the Israelites far away and encouraged them to intermarry with their new neighbors, causing family genealogical records to become extinct. This, of course, broke down their national identity.

That left the people of Judah, the southern kingdom. As prophesied by Jeremiah, they did return to their land after seventy or more years.

Their ancestry was easier to trace. And so, Nehemiah drew lots to choose one family in ten to return to Jerusalem from the outlying areas.

After |Nehemiah selected one-tenth of the people to dwell in Jerusalem, additional families volunteered to leave their established lands in outlying areas, move to Jerusalem, and adopt city life once more. That's commitment!

As per his usual humility, the man gave God proper credit for causing him to think of it.

A Time to Celebrate

After setting up a civil government, the leaders of Jerusalem realized the time was right to instruct this large group of Jewish people in methods of worship. Remember, they had been out of touch with their national identity and the Torah for decades while living in Persia. Some had little idea of what God required in his instructions to Moses so many years prior to their time.

Ezra had prepared the people of Jerusalem and surrounding cities for this important event. We can assume that during his thirteen or more years living in Jerusalem, he had spoken to them about the importance of honoring the God of their ancestors. Thus, the people knew they were embarking on an historic event this day.[38]

Nehemiah knew he could solicit help from his godly friend, Ezra. This scribe realized four elements that would get the newly settled immigrants on track again and bring about a true revival.

> 1. Sincere attention to the reading and expounding of God's Word
>
> 2. A melting of hearts and conviction of sin under the impact of the Word
>
> 3. Fasting and prayer, confession of sin, and a recognition of God's justice and mercy

4. Definite commitment to follow in the path God had marked out[39]

Ezra and more than a dozen men assembled on an elevated platform as he read from the scroll containing the Law. When he unrolled the scroll, the congregation stood to honor this timeless document. Some churches still rise in honor of God's Word when the pastor reads his text from the Bible.

Most amazing in Nehemiah's and Ezra's day is that the people stood and listened from morning until noon! Biblical scholars agree that the reading probably lasted about six hours. There were no padded pews or even chairs. What a commentary on the serious intent of these newly arrived immigrants (and on modern congregations, who become restless in padded pews after an hour and a half). This group of exiles, deprived of God's words for so long, was hungry to hear God's instructions for living. Their ignorance, a result of their ancestors' bad choices, now caused them to seek God's instructions eagerly.

Nehemiah 8:8 tells us Ezra and his platform helpers made the people "understand the reading." We can assume these recent immigrants from the Babylonian captivity spoke Chaldaic or Aramaic, popular languages during the Exile period.[40] Ezra's helpers probably translated the reading of the law into these languages and explained passages that may have been challenging to understand. Then they led their listeners in corporate worship.

Ezra may have been surprised at what came next. After he had read from early morning until noon, the entire crowd lifted up their voices and wept! Realizing their sins of ignorance as well as willful sins were offensive to God, they grieved at the laws they had broken.

And then it was the people's turn to be surprised. Ezra, Nehemiah, and the Levites turned around and instructed the people to stop crying. "Go celebrate instead!" they cried. "*Go home; eat, drink, send gifts to others;*

celebrate because you understand the words of the law!"(Nehemiah 8:9-12, my paraphrase).

These leaders knew days of fasting and mourning soon would follow. In the meantime, their celebration probably resembled our modern-day Christmas parties. They ate festively and shared with those who had nothing.

Pledging to Become Different

Nehemiah 8:13 begins the account of the people of Jerusalem and surrounding areas as they celebrated the Feast of Booths (Sukkot) for the first time in many years. This was one of three festivals when Jewish people who were able, traveled to Jerusalem to worship God and bring an offering. It occurred appropriately at the end of the harvest season. This weeklong feast commemorated the children of Israel wandering in the desert as they sought the Promised Land.

Imagine the excitement of children as their parents said, "We're going to live on the roof of our house for a week, or in our backyard, in a shelter made of sticks and branches." (What child doesn't love camping!) Some families even chose to set up booths on the street. It was a time of "very great gladness" (Nehemiah 8:17). New beginnings can be exciting.

God knows that we need rest or relaxation balanced with hard work. And though some may view Nehemiah as a no-nonsense person, this occasion demonstrated that he knew the limitations of his people. He encouraged them to rest and celebrate for a week.

Then came the eighth day of the feast. The Jewish exiles began the day with a solemn assembly, fasting and mourning. After a lengthy public prayer of praise to God and confession detailing their national unfaithfulness, the leaders called for a declaration of new rules and asked their rulers, both civil and religious, to sign the document (Nehemiah 9:38).

Commentator Adam Clarke stated, "From this sealing we learn that at this time the government of the Jews was a mixed aristocracy; composed of the nobles for the civil department, and the priests and Levites for the ecclesiastical."[41]

This led to a new beginning of faithfulness to God.

Confronting Prickly Issues

Nehemiah wasn't afraid of confrontations. There were several troublesome issues that he had to resolve, to ensure the new nation would function the way God intended. There were five main areas of concern.

1. Intermarriage with the heathen
2. Desecration of the Sabbath
3. Payment of temple tax
4. Need of fuel for the altar
5. Needs of those who ministered in the temple

You Mean I Can't Marry Just Anyone?

If these former exiles wished to maintain their national identity, they must populate the area with purely Jewish people who hadn't intermarried with the heathen. Although today some might view that as radical, Nehemiah saw it as keeping out those who might, in the future, reintroduce pagan worship practices. Those with heathen relatives might be the first to sympathize with family members who begged them to compromise just a little for the sake of keeping family peace.

Keeping the Sabbath

Unfortunately, while scattered among the Babylonians, the Jewish people absorbed their heathen lifestyle. This included treating the Sabbath just like any other day.

We experienced a welcome Sabbath sight while visiting Israel a few years ago, courtesy of kind individuals who provided the funds. We noticed a different atmosphere when the Jewish Sabbath began. Starting at 6:00 p.m. Friday and continuing through 6:00 p.m. Saturday, an air of expectancy prevailed. The hotel programmed their elevators to stop automatically at every floor, thus eliminating the need for people to press buttons or "work." Families got together and ate a leisurely evening meal; no one watched their cell phones or dashed off to other engagements.

In Nehemiah's situation, he and Ezra followed God's law given to Moses. That meant prohibiting the buying and selling on their Sabbath. What a difference in our country if those who claim Christianity would pull back from regular pursuits on our Sabbath. If we chose to eat at home instead of causing others to work at restaurants on our behalf…if sporting events occurred other days besides Sunday…if those who wished to honor God would choose other days to shop and mow lawns, the world would sit up and take notice.

Not only would these new residents of Jerusalem observe the Sabbath the way God intended, they also were required to observe the statute which caused them to forgive debts every seven years. In addition, they agreed to let the land rest every Sabbatical (seventh) year.

Caring for the Ministry

The last three changes all concerned taking care of the temple and those who worked there. The new residents of Jerusalem pledged to faithfully supply the needs of the temple and workers, including wood for the offerings, first fruits of their produce, and even their bread dough. As for the bread dough, this meant that after the grain was harvested, each household was to bring a certain amount of bread made from the first of the newly harvested grain. No one ate of this dough until it had been brought to the temple workers.

Nehemiah 12:47 details a splendid plan. The Levites (those who worked in the temple) accepted tithes from the people. Then they turned around and tithed their tithe to the priests. That way, all had their daily needs met. As long as tithes were faithfully brought to the storehouse (special rooms in the temple, designated for storage), the system worked smoothly.

The Dedication

If you ever passed by a football stadium during a game (I don't advise it; traffic is horrendous), you probably heard the roar of the crowd even before you came close to the arena. That's what the city of Jerusalem may have sounded like when the residents, as well as those from outlying areas, got together to mark the dedication of Jerusalem's wall. It was a celebration of their outstanding building project as well as the establishing of a new civil government based on God's laws. Who wouldn't be joyous!

Not only did the people shout for joy, they also formed two choirs that sang loudly, accompanied by musical instruments. One part of the people, led by Ezra, enthusiastically marched on top of the wall in one direction, while the other part, led by Nehemiah, marched in the opposite. They met in the middle, climbed down from the wall, and proceeded to the temple to offer sacrifices and praises to God. Those in outlying areas heard the joyful shouts and loud musical instruments from far away.

"Mama, what is that loud noise coming from Jerusalem?" children in outlying areas may have asked as they played outside. Probably farmers in fields miles away stopped work and strained their eyes to witness the unusual sight of a whole city celebrating. They gazed with wonder at the sight of a large crowd joyfully dancing and singing on the top of the new wall—the wall some people thought never would be built.

I like to think this unique celebration resembled the Ohio State University Marching Band at a half-time show. No, I haven't been there, but I've seen pictures and heard recordings of their show-stopping performances. Joyous music, beautiful harmony, and high-stepping marchers—the Israelites had it all.

Did you ever wonder if Tobiah dropped his gaze in embarrassment that day? During his intimidation efforts, he sarcastically commented that a fox would break down the Jews' flimsy wall. Now it held a large group of people: two choirs plus city officials marching on top of it. They knew the God of the Israelites indeed had fulfilled His promise given in Jeremiah 29:10: For thus saith the Lord, That after seventy years be accomplished at Babylon I will visit you, and perform my good word toward you, in causing you to return to this place. For I know the thoughts that I think toward you, saith the Lord, thoughts of peace, and not of evil, to give you an expected end.

You can read about it in Nehemiah 12:27-43.

The Nehemiah Principle

Nehemiah and Ezra realized that in choosing leaders for God's work, it is vitally important to select those with character first. Skills can be developed; character and personal influence should be foremost. Both Hanani and Hananiah exhibited admirable character traits.

How does this translate into practice in our day? According to page 121 of the course "Ministry Leadership" in *Shepherds Global Classroom* (www.shepherdsglobalclassroom.org 2016), "A church should train people to know how to greet a visitor, how to pray with someone at the altar, what discipleship to offer to a new convert, how to respond to a material need in the congregation, and many other practices." The pastor who takes this challenge seriously will save grief in the future when he might otherwise find it necessary to remediate past faulty practices.

Those interested in further instruction for pastoral leadership would benefit from reading the entirety of chapter thirteen of the course mentioned above.

Living God's way produces not only peace, but also joy. Conforming to new ways of behavior requires total commitment. Those who determine to obey God, no matter the cost, find cause for great celebration privately and collectively.

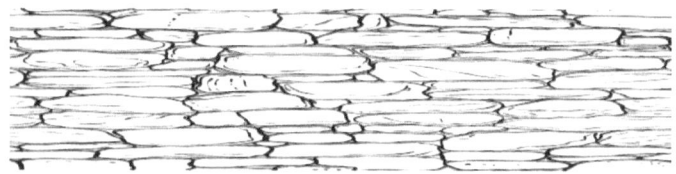

Dear Father in heaven, You are so patient and so gracious to Your children when they take a step of obedience. Please help me relay that message often to those in my congregation. In the name of your Son, the fountain of joy, amen.

CHAPTER ELEVEN

Worship in Theory and Practice

Siblings Karla and Kaylee moved from the conservative Midwest to a city in the East. After settling in, they sought a church family. Several congregations left them perplexed at the styles of worship they encountered. When one pastor appeared on the platform in jeans and a t-shirt, Kaylee said, "Would he would dress that way if he were a guest of the President at the White House?"

They tried another church. It featured people slurping drinks from soda cans during the service. Karla thought, if my boyfriend were trying to convince me he adored me just before proposing, and if he got down on one knee while gulping Mountain Dew and checking his cell phone, would I think he was serious? This was her mental picture of their casual approach to worshipping the God of majesty.

A third congregation featured a worship style they liked—except for one thing. After a few congregational songs, the pastor stopped the service and told everyone to go around and shake hands with others. This meet-and-greet exercise made Kaylee, the introvert, uncomfortable. She enjoyed the service otherwise, but wondered why they would interrupt people's heavenward thoughts and guide them, instead, in a horizontal direction.

The siblings chose the third church but planned on arriving after the song service ended. The meet-and-greet experience felt like overkill when people already greeted one another as they entered and exited the building. Unfortunately, the girls missed a vital component of worship: singing praises to God.

Worship styles vary as much as the people planning them. Older ministers describe services where the shekinah glory appeared so real that people were afraid to move. (The word *shekinah* doesn't appear in the

Bible, but in Hebrew it signifies God's presence that dwells or settles over people.) In parts of the last century, God's convicting presence in church services was so strong it arrested sinners and caused them to tremble and grip the backs of the pews.

As the social revolution of the 1960s and '70s grew, churches experienced a decline in the awareness of God's presence. Some turned to a *seeker-friendly* approach, bringing people to church on buses and serving refreshments. The goal? Making outsiders feel comfortable and happy. While community outreach can impact outsiders, what do we, the church, offer them when they walk through our doors?

Today's pastor faces the challenge of ministering to multiple generations with conflicting views of worship. In Nehemiah chapter eight, we find a comparable situation.

Those who recently returned from the Babylonian exile had been deprived of the complete knowledge of God and His requirements for worship for over seventy years. Some may not have known that the God of the Hebrews even *had* requirements. Ezra the scribe and Nehemiah the governor had the responsibility of establishing proper protocol.

Pastors in the twenty-first century experienced a similar situation after the COVID-19 pandemic. Churches deprived of the right to gather in corporate worship began congregating once more. But would they need to adjust their approach to public services?

Several years ago, we were privileged to know one of the saintliest men in our circle of friends. His approach to worship was unique and resulted in an awe-inspiring sense of God's presence in our church.

Rev. Miles was a retired minister with a dignified demeaner and a British accent. Those visiting in his home felt ushered into a peaceful, heavenly presence. The man's deep prayer life made the difference. As a result, we noticed how he chose to worship.

His was a vertical approach instead of a horizontal one. When arriving at church, this devoted saint walked directly to his seat, bowed his head, and quietly prayed. If he passed others in the aisle he smiled politely and nodded hello, yet deferred carrying on conversation. One look at his countenance told us he had been dwelling in God's presence before he arrived. He never appeared unkind or unfriendly, just devoted to fellowshipping with God first.

After the worship service was over, Rev. Miles went back into horizontal mode, pleasantly speaking to those around him in his impeccable British accent. Yet, his prayer life and reverent demeanor helped set the atmosphere for the Spirit of God to pervade time and again. I will insert a personal preference here, yet I think it worthy of consideration. In contrast to the above example, the meet-and-greet practice in the middle of the service, adopted by many churches today, sometimes frustrates shy, introverted people. While extroverts thrive on human contact, introverted people can view the forced socialization as either annoying or overwhelming. Perhaps pastors could take an informal vote among their own flock. They might be surprised that many would choose to forego the socialization exercise.

I am deeply indebted to Dr. Randall McElwain for permission to glean insights from his series of messages on the topic of worship, which you can read below. Much of the remainder of this chapter reflects those thoughts.

Let's look at the components of worship. We will consider:
- What happens when we worship
- Worship as evangelism
- Old and New Testament principles of worship
- Worship, from theory to practice

What Happens When We Worship?

Did you ever think about what happens when we worship? First, we see God. A New Testament word for *worship* means, "to bow down or fall down in humility and awe." In Old English, the word can translate, "Give to the king the honor he deserves or is worthy of: *worth-ship*."

It's not about seeing ourselves. We tend to evaluate a worship service by what we get out of it. Instead, we should evaluate it by what we give to God, the One who is high and lifted up.

Worship doesn't start with us. We don't say, "Okay, God, we're assembled here to worship you now." Instead, it is God saying to us, "I am inviting you through grace into My presence."

Contrary to man's sometimes-faulty thinking, God is not a celestial Santa Claus or a soda pop machine. We don't serve Him because He makes us feel good or gives us what we want. Worship is not entertainment; it's proactive.

We sometimes approach God as children carelessly playing with a stick of dynamite. He is, after all, *power* and *might*. Hebrews 12:21-23 speaks of coming into the presence of the Judge of all the earth. We don't have to wait until we get to heaven to come into His presence. We are in His presence when we worship *now*.

Worship is not about satisfying our musical tastes. It's not about feeling good about ourselves or socializing with friends, though fellowship is important. It is reverence for the God who is a consuming fire, the One Moses encountered on the sacred mountain.

Strong's Hebrew Lexicon defines worship as "the act of rising to a personal ... consciousness of the real presence of God, which floods the soul with joy and bathes the whole inward spirit with refreshing streams of life."[42] At the dedication of Solomon's temple, God's presence was so powerful that the priests couldn't continue their tasks (II Chronicles 5:13, 14).

After we see God in worship, we then see ourselves. The prophet Isaiah saw the Lord "high and lifted up," then saw *himself* as God saw him. What a contrast! In true worship, we see God's holiness and then our desperate need for His ongoing grace.

Thirdly, in true worship we are changed. The prophet Isaiah saw himself as unclean. True worship always leads to a transformation. It changed Isaiah. It changed the Samaritan woman at the well. True worship will change you and me on Sunday at our local church. Do we live differently after leaving a church service?

Worship that fails to transform lives is not true worship.

What are the results in worship when lives are *not* transformed? The lowly prophet Amos delivered God's response to a self-satisfied people who refused to abandon their sins, even though they followed prescribed worship practices. In today's vernacular, God might have said, "Cancel the choir rehearsal; send the musicians home; I don't want to hear any more."

Why? Israel in Amos's day was following correct rituals, even sacrificing to the true God. But when they went home, worship had not changed their lives; they still took bribes. Their worship was empty. God implied, "Don't bother coming back."

Continuing the role of worship, we view the Corinthian church in the apostle Paul's day.

This group of believers had exciting services with manifestations of various spiritual gifts. But the church tolerated open sin. If we continue in willful sin on Monday, we did not truly worship on Sunday. We felt only an emotional response.

Coming a little closer (and perhaps uncomfortably), we should ask ourselves, "In service, what do I do when the Spirit of God whispers, "You need to apologize to that person across the aisle"? Do we pull out our cell phones and drown out the voice of God?

Obeying the prompts of the Holy Spirit can tear down walls of conflict within the local church. One congregation was divided over—as ridiculous as this seems—the color of the new carpet they needed for the sanctuary. Families took sides. Friendships were strained. During one worship service, however (probably after much prayer), things took a different turn. The Spirit of God began softening hearts. People saw themselves as God saw them, steeped in animosity and rebellion. One man walked across the aisle to his old friend whom he had treated coldly. He apologized and asked forgiveness. Broken, they both shed tears.

The obedience of one man prompted a break in the service. Others walked across the aisle and apologized. And, to the pastor's relief, true worship and obedience followed.

Proper worship changed John Wesley's life as well as his motivation when he saw himself in relation to the God of heaven. Wesley's conversion proved pivotal to his success as a minister. We read that he attended a meeting on Aldersgate Street one night, heard Luther's preface to the Epistle of Romans, and felt his heart strangely warmed. What we may not realize, however, is that earlier that day, Wesley visited St. Peter's Cathedral. While there he thought about failures in his personal life and his missionary endeavors. He heard the choir anthem, "Out of the depths I cry to Thee," and the thoughts continued in Wesley's mind, "for with the Lord is steadfast love and plentiful redemption." Wesley spent the day pondering those contemplations. He was ready to worship that night because a view of God's holiness had changed him.

Evangelistic Worship

The book of Acts begins with worship and ends with evangelism. In reading Acts chapter two, we notice those in the upper room at Pentecost immediately began evangelizing when they were filled with the Holy Spirit. *Worship inspires evangelism.* The calling of Paul and Barnabas came during worship. When we see God, we will want to bring our friends and neighbors to meet Him.

Because the prophet Isaiah worshipped (Isaiah 6:8), he could say, "Here am I; send me." We cannot separate worship and evangelism. As we worship, we see our world as God sees it. We glimpse sinners and gain a heart of evangelism. We are no longer satisfied just to gather in our four walls.

Isaiah's ministry was marked by rejection. God warned him that his message would not be accepted by those around him. After Isaiah's faithful decades of preaching, wicked king Manasseh put him to death. Why, then, would Isaiah preach? God wasn't calling him for human approval. He saw a Holy God, full of majesty, who deserved his very best.

Ministry can be hard and thankless. Missionaries often see few results for their labor. Therefore, everything Christian workers do must be related to the worship of God, whether serving as Sunday school teachers, outreach persons, or pastors. Keeping our sight on God can make the most challenging aspects of ministry less formidable.

The Lord nudged a pastor's wife once about keeping a mindset of worship during the Sunday morning services. She had been hurriedly scribbling their tithe check while the ushers passed the offering plates. A view of God that day reminded her that her actions smacked of last-minute, thoughtless haste. From that point on, she made a point to have their tithe check written and tucked into her purse on Saturday night.

In Acts 16, we read that Paul and Silas were worshipping God at midnight when fellow prisoners heard them. One writer illustrated it with the following story. Since I couldn't locate the original author, I have rewritten it in my own words.

* * *

You thought you were having a bad day. Paul and Silas could have written a book about their experience in the city of Philippi. Actually, one author *did* write about it in chapter sixteen of the book of Acts.

In just one day, the two missionaries had cast a demon out of an oppressed girl, faced false accusations from a jealous mob, found themselves arrested and dragged through the streets, stripped out of their clothes, beaten with many stripes, and thrown into prison. Then they found themselves in chains in a dark dungeon with rats probably nibbling at their toes.

You and I may have slumped on that cold, dirty floor and wished we could call a lawyer. We may have reminded the Lord how we were suffering for Him. What did Paul and Silas do?

They opened their mouths wide and sang robust praises to God! They reckoned their suffering to be light, compared to their reward in heaven.

God smiles when His children pray and sing when they would rather indulge in anger or self-pity. He delights when we supply a glad surrender to His ways. He alone is aware of the results of our trials and afflictions.

When Paul and Silas performed their impromptu concert on the floor of their dark dungeon, the earth shook so violently that *all* the prison doors swung open. *All* the chains broke. Sleepers awakened and listened.

A sacrifice of praise brings God to his feet, applauding. When God stands up and claps, chains snap. Hearts cry, "Show us your Jesus!"

So, if we find ourselves in a dungeon, God calls us to sing. That's evangelistic worship.

Joyful Worship Draws Visitors

A thoughtful person noted that when choosing a restaurant, "A happy customer is a better advertisement than a half-page ad in the newspaper." The same is true for the church.

What does jubilant worship look like? Some of the most uplifting services we have attended have been those with joyful congregations singing and then joining in fervent prayers. This set the tone for a deep, inspiring message from the pastor. Of course, not all services will be upbeat in nature. Sometimes the man of God must remind his people of God's judgment on willful and hidden sin. However, what we call the *preliminaries* (congregational singing, announcements, collecting the offerings, special music, corporate prayer), when presented joyfully, can set the atmosphere for the Word of God to sink deep into prepared hearts and minds.

God impressed David to build the Gentiles' court around the temple so the heathen would overhear and be drawn to worship his God. In II Samuel 22:50, David sang, "I will give thanks unto thee, O Lord, *among the heathen.*" David realized that praising the God who answered the prayers of his people could turn other nations to that One also.

Principles of Worship in the Bible

We have seen from the book of Amos that true worship comes from an obedient heart.

The first time we see the word *worship* in the English Bible is in Genesis 22:5. Abraham's willingness to sacrifice Isaac was a supreme act of worship. When Moses wrote about it later, he put special emphasis on the details of Abraham's obedience. God's instructions to Abraham were *specific* and *costly.*

An obedient heart changes when God tells it to change. It is a heart that says, "I will not argue or negotiate with God. I will obey, even if it's in a church service. It doesn't even have to be an altar call."

Obedience is possible only through God's grace.

In Genesis chapter three, we read of God walking through the Garden of Eden, taking the initiative to speak with Adam and Eve. His original intent was unbroken fellowship between man and his Creator.

Worship can be a way of celebrating God's grace. Note that Abraham chose to build altars in places where God revealed himself. He wanted to remember those places. The heathen, by contrast, built altars to try to please their gods, to win their favor. Abraham's altars, instead, were a way of celebrating God's grace.

The book of Leviticus tells us how a fallen people can approach a perfectly holy God.

First, we notice a *seeker-friendly* approach focuses on the wrong person. (Think donuts and basketball in the youth pavilion on Sunday morning.) A better way is to invite God into our midst instead. Make *Him* welcome.

Jacob's worship in Genesis is a study in paradox. When we think of Jacob in the Old Testament we get a picture of a heel-grabbing cheater, running to escape the problems he created. Despite Jacob's problems, God made it possible for this rogue to worship. Only through grace does God invite us into His presence, even when we don't deserve it.

Another Old Testament example is in II Chronicles 30, when King Hezekiah wanted to restore the Passover. Backstory: seven years after the Northern Kingdom fell to Assyria, Hezekiah restored the temple and invited survivors of the invasion to come to Jerusalem and join the Passover. Many laughed and scorned. But the men of Asher, Manasseh and Zebulun came.

Unfortunately, not all the men prepared themselves. These former captives had lost God's rules for worship while living in a foreign nation. Ignorant of God's prescribed methods, they ate the Passover feast without properly preparing themselves.

Hezekiah realized this may have been due to their ignorance. He prayed and asked God to pardon those who offended. The result? God in grace accepted their worship.

On this occasion God viewed them as a father would look at a simple crayon drawing from his four-year-old child. Knowing it came from hearts that wanted to give their best, God overlooked it. He says to us also in essence, "You give what you can; I'll make up the difference." We worship in grace.

An Audience of One

The twelfth chapter of the book of John tells the story of Mary breaking an alabaster box of oil and using its contents to anoint the feet of Jesus. The disciples called it wasteful. Jesus called it worship.

In the world's eyes, worship is a waste, but Jesus says it's beautiful. It's not trying to make a deal with God; instead, it's pure adoration with no strings attached.

God requires our best in worship. The Old Testament priests had to be scrupulous as they carried out their duties. If God required the same today, how many pastors might lose their lives? It is serious business, since *how* we worship reflects *why* we worship.

Let's look at other examples from the Bible. Cain was required to worship by sacrifice but didn't follow instructions. He did it his own way with disastrous results. Abel, his brother, brought the right offering with the right reason. By faith, he brought what God required.

In the book of Malachi, we see that people brought lame animals for sacrifice, instead of their best. Like Cain, they "worshipped" with the wrong motives.

In Exodus 26, we see the building of the tabernacle required many details. Fourteen times in Exodus we see they "did as the Lord commanded Moses." They paid attention to God's requirements.

In Exodus 36, we see that when people gave for the furnishings of the new tabernacle, they offered so much that Moses had to tell them to stop. The people had joy in giving.

Considering the above, how can we be careful in our worship today?

When we worship from obedient hearts, no musician will say, "I didn't have time to practice this week." No Sunday school teacher will be unprepared. We won't be scrolling through Facebook—or any social media—during the service. King David had the right idea when he refused to give a sacrifice that cost him nothing. We can do no less.

True worship has an audience of one. Unfortunately, many come to worship services thinking it works like a football game. The pastor represents the twenty-two players running down the field while 85,000 fans sit in the stands, eating hot dogs and watching. We should be participating in the game with *God* as the audience, not us. Worship is not entertainment.

Worship Is Proactive

In the Old Testament tabernacle, everyone was actively involved in worship. There were no padded pews or chairs. The worshipers laid hands on the burnt offering and killed it. They were involved in every step. Today, perhaps we should apologize to God instead of to people in the congregation, for limping along with little or no preparation.

A music director faced a unique challenge. Rory, an older man, desperately wanted to be involved in the church choir. The problem came when the director realized Rory couldn't carry a tune. Yet, to this untrained man, singing in the choir was the ultimate way he could praise God. So, they developed a plan. The music director allowed the elderly man to "sing" with the choir. When the director heard him getting too far off tune, he signaled to Rory, and the man just mouthed the words. His heart was in the right place, even though his vocal cords didn't cooperate. This concession allowed one lonely man to become proactive in worship in a way meaningful to himself.

Back to the story of Mary in Matthew 26. No one in the room was impressed by her actions because they didn't benefit from them personally. In fact, Judas left to betray Jesus soon after this incident. Mary, on the other hand, worshiped for *an audience of one*.

Worship: Moving from Theory to Practice

Worship actually begins before we get to church. Psalms 120-134, called Songs of Ascent, were sung by travelers as they walked in groups to Jerusalem once a year, singing as they went. They set a great example for us today.

Those climbing the hill towards Jerusalem anticipated the thrill of going to God's house. We must prepare ahead of time and anticipate God's presence with the thought, "I will obey You, Lord." An old minister friend used to say, "We can spoil our Sunday morning worship by what we do Saturday night." He meant, of course, staying up late Saturday night could make our minds lack sharpness, and have trouble focusing.

We see also, the worshipers entered God's house with joy. Many had walked from Galilee in the north, to the temple in Jerusalem. Psalm 126 expresses the delight the former exiles felt when returning from that sacred experience. The heathen said, "Look how happy their worship makes them!"

Next, *they brought sacrifices and listened with wonder and awe* as the priest read Scripture. It was a solemn moment. Today, the prelude or call to worship sets the tone for our service. John Wesley sometimes stopped people after they sang a hymn and asked, "Do these words ring true to you?"

Announcements can be part of encouragement to join in the life of the church. Corporate prayer carries us into the presence of God. Giving an offering is a type of worship. Note: one missionary pastor noticed a difference in attitudes when he changed from saying, "It's time to *take* the offering," to, "It's time to *give our* offering." That indicated to his congregation his proactive approach.

Another component of preliminary worship is music. It allows God to speak to us in yet another way. Unfortunately, the advent of contemporary Christian music has shaped many congregations into spectator-type worshipers instead of active participants. The reason? Contemporary music is challenging to follow. Instead of singing along to unfamiliar words and tunes, many just watch. They are like football fans sitting in the stadium. And music with a throbbing beat appeals to the flesh and turns our attention the wrong direction.

During the days when timeless, majestic hymns were written, those grand anthems taught solid doctrine to churchgoers. They drew attention to God's attributes instead of being spliced with frequent references to "I" and "me." Can we do no less?

While some contemporary worship songs exhibit the three components of quality music (melody, harmony, and rhythm), worship benefits the most when these three elements are kept in balance. Songs heavy on rhythm produce a sensuous effect. Songs with frequent references to "I" and "me" create an emotional, sentimental atmosphere. We must remember to draw attention to the God of heaven in all we do during the service.

Continuing in worship, the sermon should not only remind us of God's great attributes as well as his love for us, but also should stir us out of our lethargy. Praying for the pastor while he preaches is a good idea; it helps him and us stay focused. God often speaks in whispers. We must listen intentionally.

As the minister opens the Word and explains it, there should be evidence that he studied and prayed over the message. No dry college lecture, no texting or checking cell phones, no wandering minds can substitute for an anointed experience of sensing God's presence in our midst.

Lastly, we see that worship continues on Monday. The way we live on Monday tells a great deal about whether we worshiped on Sunday. Hebrews 10:25 exhorts us to not forsake assembling with others in corporate worship. We need each other.

Of course, not all corporate worship in the early New Testament resembled Pentecost in the second chapter of Acts. Rushing wind and fire probably weren't the norm. Yet today, it's not about mindlessly going through the program while we plan Sunday's meal or make a mental to-do list for the next day. Life can be different on Monday because of our worship on Sunday.

Worship in Heaven

Those familiar with Mark Twain's book, *The Adventures of Huckleberry Finn,* probably noticed Miss Watson's impression of heaven. This simple woman tells Huck that there is a "good place" to go where all anyone has to do is sit around with a harp and sing forever. That sounded boring to a boy with an abundance of energy.

Twain's concept of heaven probably explains why he lived like he didn't care to go there.

Actually, in heaven, we will spend eternity in a life of worship. And it won't be boring. Let's take some cues from the Apostle John's revelation of heaven.

In the book of Revelation, chapter one, we see John exiled on the island of Patmos. Most Bible scholars feel it was due to his preaching about Jesus. On this lonely, rocky island, John was worshiping privately on the Lord's Day when Jesus appeared behind him and spoke. John turned around and saw The Living Word of God in all His glory and splendor. He looked for the Lion of Judah and instead saw the sacrificial Lamb who restored our fellowship with God.

In chapter four of Revelation, the scene moves to heaven, and reveals a picture of what is happening there. The worship in heaven centers on God, the One who sits on His throne. Just as in Isaiah chapter six, the focus is on God's power, glory, and honor (Revelation 4:1). This was especially comforting to the early church. It gave them a picture of what it would be like when they no longer had to endure persecution. Their worship was not about how it made them feel about themselves or their circumstances, but instead it focused on God.

Revelation chapter five reminds us that though God's plan for fellowship with man was interrupted in the Garden, it will resume in heaven. Worship in heaven is an eternal celebration of the fact that the Lamb who was slain is victorious, having accomplished God's eternal purpose: reconciliation of God and man.

Revelation chapters six and seven remind us that even though chaos was reigning on earth, the people in heaven continued to worship. The Apostle John's letter to people persecuted by the Roman emperor Caesar, was in essence saying, "Yes, it looks bad down here. But I want you to see the victorious, triumphant worship that has already started. Someday we get to join it." John's letter reminds us today that in the worst times of trouble, we must not focus on the disturbing events around us, but on the One who sits on the throne. *When worship is most difficult for us, it also is most important.*

Many people—especially those with small children—arrive at church with scattered thoughts. Parents arrive still trying to put shoes on their toddler and find change for little Johnny's Sunday school offering. Older saints wonder why the car was hard to start. It's hard to pull our attention away from the earthly all around us. A well thought-out plan of worship draws our focus heavenward and reminds us of God's wonderful attributes. Before the fall of man in the Garden, worship consisted of intimate fellowship between God and man. Worship was then and will be in heaven a life centered on unbroken fellowship with God for eternity. Revelation chapter 21 is a return to Genesis chapter three. God will dwell with us, and we will be His people.

I'm looking forward to that, aren't you?

Here is a poem Charles Spurgeon wrote after observing those attending church.

Some go to church to take a walk;
Some go there to laugh and talk.
Some go there to meet a friend;
Some go there their time to spend.
Some go there to meet a lover;
Some go there a fault to cover.
Some go there for speculation;
Some go there for observation.
Some go there to doze and nod;
The wise go there to worship God.[43]

The Nehemiah Principle

We have seen in this chapter that:

- Worship is proactive.
- It begins before we get to church.
- Joyful worship attracts others.
- We are to actively participate.
- Worship on Sunday affects how we live the rest of the week.
- True worship changes lives.

Nehemiah and Ezra helped their exiled Jewish kinsmen and women to return to a meaningful system of worship. The events of chapters eight, nine, and ten of the book of Nehemiah represent worship in its finest form. Its elements included:

- Conviction of a deep-seated tendency toward sinfulness and disobedience
- A godly sorrow for, and confession of, sin
- A recognition of the holiness of God, manifested in the righteousness and mercy of all His dealings with man
- A total commitment or consecration of oneself to God in faith, trusting that with His help it is possible to live a life free from sin[44]

Note, also, that the worship instituted in Ezra's and Nehemiah's day became proactive. The citizens involved in Jerusalem realized it was serious business. Though they were joyful at times; they also became solemn when carrying out their obligations to God.

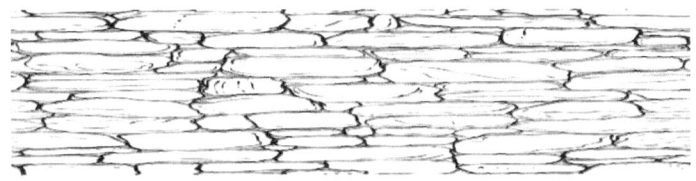

Dear Heavenly Father, You have made it possible for us to worship You through the sacrifice of Your Son. Thank you for revealing Yourself to us through Jesus Christ. We know that when we give You our worship, You give Yourself to us more and more. Our reward is a deepening and a more meaningful relationship with the King of kings and Lord of lords. We look forward to the day when that worship will be continued in heaven, for all eternity. All because of Jesus, amen.

CHAPTER TWELVE

Contending with Your Tobiah

Pastor Nate inherited an unusual problem when he agreed to shepherd a small, struggling church. The congregation owned an apartment where a woman had lived rent-free for a very long time. Each month she escaped her obligation to pay rent and seemed to have no intentions of changing her lucrative habit. You can read more about Nate's "Tobiah" later in this chapter.

God's servant, Nehemiah, inherited a similar issue after his return to check on the "state of the union" in Jerusalem. Having traveled back to Persia, possibly to resume his job as the king's cupbearer, he saw reason to travel once more to Jerusalem. His mission: to survey the progress of the reforms he and Ezra instituted.

Arriving in the city where he had invested twelve years as governor, Nehemiah experienced shock and grief. Jerusalem was in a state of decay, so very different than the city he left behind.

The Walls Held Firm but the Moral Climate Crumbled

One of the most disgusting things Nehemiah found was his archenemy, Tobiah, living in a spacious apartment in the temple area. The rooms Tobiah occupied were intended to hold temple treasures, as well as food for the workers. Instead, this blasphemer resided in luxury in a suite of rooms set apart for use by the priests and Levites.

How did this come about? Family ties. Remember the reference to families in chapter five? The ties that bind or gag? This was an antithesis to the kinship factor that enabled Nehemiah earlier, to enlist workers to build nearest to their family dwellings.

Family loyalty can be a good thing—or a bad thing. Eliashib, smug in his role as high priest, used it as an occasion to pad the lives of his relatives. Eliashib and Tobiah were related by marriage. In fact, before Nehemiah left Jerusalem the first time, Tobiah's cronies kept the mocker informed of Nehemiah's activities. In addition, one of Eliashib's grandsons was son-in-law to Sanballat, Tobiah's old partner in taunting the Jewish people.

Nehemiah's fiery zeal for the house of God caused an immediate, godly reaction. Yes, *godly* reaction. Remember, one side of God's holy character is love, the other is judgment. Acting in hot exuberance for God's laws, Nehemiah threw all Tobiah's belongings out of the temple. *All* his belongings. Then he commanded those rooms to be thoroughly cleansed. A spring cleaning, if you will.

One commentator said, "Sin must have a radical cure. It is not a thing to be condoned, and especially when it manifests itself in the heart or life of a professed saint of God. It must be purged away as if by fire, if the individual is to maintain his integrity with God or regain the favor he has lost."[45] Eliashib, as high priest, compromised his position; Nehemiah felt no hesitation to override the man's sinful decisions.

We note that Nehemiah didn't even have to pray about this situation before taking action. The description in Nehemiah 13:5-9 tells us he acted *immediately*. For those who appear shocked at such radical behavior, the Beacon Bible Commentary offers this insight: "The reforms described in this last chapter of Nehemiah are achieved in a spirit that suggests Jesus' manner in cleansing the temple or in dealing with Pharisees who abused the law of Moses, although professing to follow it.[46]

Remember Pastor Nate's unwelcomed tenant at the beginning of this chapter? Let's see what happened when he took similar action. Here is the story he shared with us.

Sending In the Bulldog

We moved to a new pastorate where the church was small and struggling. The parsonage was a duplex, and the church was supposed to be renting out one side to help with finances.

Notice, I said *supposed to be* charging rent for the place next door. This venture was unsuccessful on our part.

It started before I arrived as pastor. The problem was a single lady with two children living in the other side of the duplex. She hadn't paid her rent in a very long time. Former pastors had appealed to her with no success. These leaders simply didn't follow up with their demands. That may have been what motivated our denomination to send "The Bulldog" (me) to remedy the thorny situation.

After we lived there six months—and our tenant still hadn't paid her rent—I knocked on her door one day. I told her she had one month to pay her rent, or I was changing the locks on her doors—and she wouldn't be getting the keys. Whatever possessions were in her apartment would be mine.

The day before the month was up, our tenant sent her son over to tell me she didn't have the money and couldn't get out. He was incredulous that we would actually follow through with our warning. That's when it became interesting.

With a smile I said that was okay, but by the end of the next day I would be changing the locks and whatever was left in the house would be mine.

We were amazed at the sudden motivation this tenant showed when someone finally stood their ground. I wasn't unkind—I even smiled when I gave the ultimatum. The lady apparently had little experience with boundaries.

During the middle of the night, this woman who had taken advantage of Christian charity for so long, had a friend come over and help her move all her belongings. The next day we changed the locks.

So many times, Christians fear that if we stand firm on an issue, people won't like our Jesus. In James 4:7, we are told to "resist the devil and he will flee from you." While there are times to show Christian charity, there also are times to recognize when Satan is taking advantage of our timidity. It worked in Nehemiah's day. Our experience proved it will work in this day, too.

Why Is the House of God Forsaken?

The second issue Nehemiah found was abuses of offerings. Apparently, the people had neglected to bring in their tithes as promised. Consequently, the Levites and singers had to move to the country or suburbs and make a living by farming. If the people had brought in their tithes as directed, the singers and Levites could have made their living solely by working in the temple. Nehemiah called together the leaders and set things straight. He delegated dependable men to distribute faithfully to their brethren, the temple workers (Nehemiah 13:13).

Restoring Sabbath Observance

Moving past the first two abuses, Nehemiah then set straight the Sabbath desecration that took place during his absence. People in Jerusalem were treating their Sabbath like all other days, buying and selling and conducting regular business. Outsiders from Tyre, north of Jerusalem, were bringing in fish and other wares and selling them to Jewish residents on the day God commanded should be kept holy.

Again, Nehemiah took the matter to Jerusalem's leaders. He reminded them that the same trespass they allowed had brought God's judgment on Jerusalem in the first place. (Think Babylonian captivity.) Knowing they possibly might slip around and continue their disobedience, Nehemiah ordered his own guards to stand at the gates at sundown Friday night until sundown Saturday (the parameters of the Jewish Sabbath).

After Nehemiah corrected this blatant disregard for God's commands, merchants tried a different trick. These sellers of wares lodged outside the gates a few times, hoping Jerusalem's residents would come out to them. Nehemiah saw through this ruse and spoke to them directly. "Why lodge ye about the wall? If ye do so again, I will lay hands on you" (Nehemiah 13:21). By this time his reputation was well established. Even those outside Jerusalem heard that Nehemiah meant what he said. And they didn't want to risk getting beaten, literally.

The Stickiest Subject of All

The last reform Nehemiah tackled was the one that caused him to gain more of a reputation than he already possessed. Nehemiah 13:23–30 tells the story of this great reformer's radical behavior when he discovered the people—including the priests—had taken wives from the heathen nations of Ashdod and Ammon and Moab. He discovered (v. 24) that the children reared in these Jewish homes couldn't even speak the Jews' language! How then could they understand the reading of the Torah?

In an outcry for this blatant disregard of their previous vows, Nehemiah approached the guilty, and contended with them. Commentator Adam Clarke offers a unique perspective of Nehemiah's actions.

> Verse 25. *I contended with them*—Proved the fact against these iniquitous fathers, in a legal assembly.

And cursed them—Denounced the judgments of God and the sentence of the law upon them.

Smote certain of them—Had them punished by whipping.

And plucked off their hair—Had them shaven, as a mark of the greatest ignominy.

And made them swear by God, saying, Ye shall not give—Caused them to bind themselves by an oath, that they would make no intermarriages with those who were not of the seed of Israel.[47]

The *British Family Bible* Commentary sheds historical background on this unusual practice described in Nehemiah 13:25.

And cursed them—Denounced the curses of God which would fall upon them if they did not reform (Dr. Wells).

And smote certain of them &c—Ordered the publick (sic) officers to beat some of the most notorious offenders with rods or scourges, according to De 25:2; "and plucked off their hair." This punishment was esteemed a peculiar disgrace in Eastern countries; Isa. 50:6; Jer. 48:37. The hair was reckoned a great ornament, and a distinction of a free man; thus, to pluck it off was to brand a person with shame, and to give him the appearance of a slave (Bp. Patrick).

The proper meaning of the Hebrew word is, that they tore off the hair with violence, which punishment was painful as well as disgraceful. This kind of punishment was common in Persia (Calmet).[48]

Spurgeon Devotional Commentary states this insight into Nehemiah's vigorous behavior: "This stern ruler saw that the mixed marriages placed the whole nation in jeopardy, and therefore he was indignant. Love of his country made him intolerant of that which would prove its ruin."[49]

Clearly, Nehemiah didn't just cry out against wrong; he always provided a permanent solution and followed that with prayer.

Now let's see one last instance of a modern-day pastor who reacted and corrected an ongoing wrong in his congregation. Here is the story in his own words.

A Time for Righteous Indignation

One of the main things any pastor wants is for his congregation to grow. However, this takes people, and people tend to come just as they are. This translates into the reality that some people and situations require much patience, along with grace and tact. Unfortunately, in some places, these values are in short supply.

In one of my pastorates a particular family had started to attend, and when they did, other relatives of theirs began to come. Then the parents of the second family, who had been attending a more nominal church, but who were trying to encourage their children and grandchildren to draw closer to God, started attending as well. Admittedly, their outward dress standards were different than most in our church. But, when you consider where they were coming from, you would think that anyone would be able to see they were moving in the right direction.

Both the husband and wife in this family obviously loved God, and loved our church. They would frequently testify during services. The spirit of their testimonies was far better than some who had been entrenched in the church for years. But suddenly, they stopped attending. Puzzled, I went to visit. That's when I found that someone in our church (they graciously declined to tell me who) had told them that they should not be getting up to testify when they had different outward standards of dress than most of our group. They were understandably hurt and never came back to our church again.

As the pastor, I found this situation terribly upsetting. On one hand, I felt I had a serious issue that needed to be addressed. On the other, I did not know the person responsible for offending them, so I could not go to them personally.

Another factor was that we livestreamed our services. I knew there were people all over the country who would tune in and be aware of anything I said from the pulpit. I prayed about this situation for a while, and finally concluded this was something I could not let go. I had to find a way to address it.

From time to time, we had issues with our broadcast and the service would go down. So, one Sunday evening I pre-planned with the sound booth to shut down the livestream with no explanation, right after the preliminaries. I then left the pulpit and came down into the center aisle. I explained to the congregation that I had something very serious to talk to them about that night.

I shared what had happened. I told them if I knew who had gone to these dear people, I would have come to the confronters personally and no one else ever would have known. But, since that was not an option, I still felt the matter was serious enough to warrant addressing. I wanted the whole church to know exactly how I felt about the situation.

I never did find out who went to them, but that evening, I cleared my heart about the matter to the whole congregation. We talked about how wrong that type of spirit is, how damaging it can be to the church, and ultimately, what would be the right response if ever we were so fortunate as to have outside people coming to our church again.

Some were a little taken aback by my direct, public approach. (As it turned out there was one other time during my ministry at that church where I did the same thing.) But gratifying to me, some years later I visited the area and happened to speak with a former parishioner. He said to me, "Do you remember when you shut the livestream down and had those 'Come to Jesus meetings' with us? I miss that because that was exactly what we needed." I don't know how orthodox it was, but I believe there are times when the pastor must deal with issues. He needs to not only bathe the matter in prayer, but also to display a holy boldness.

Former president Theodore Roosevelt left us with wise words about the need for righteous leaders. Below are his words:

It is not the critic who counts; not the man who points out how the strong man stumbles, or where the doer of deeds could have done them better. The credit belongs to the man who is actually in the arena, whose face is marred by dust and sweat and blood; who strives valiantly; who errs, who comes short again and again, because there is no effort without error and shortcoming; but who does actually strive to do the deeds; who knows great enthusiasms, the great devotions; who spends himself in a worthy cause; who at the best knows in the end the triumph of high achievement, and who at the worst, if he fails, at least fails while daring greatly, so that his place shall never be with those cold and timid souls who neither know victory nor defeat.

The Nehemiah Principle

Have you noticed how often Nehemiah said he contended with someone? He was not afraid of confrontations. His actions might be considered outlandish or rash by today's watered-down standards of behavior. But Nehemiah was a man of vision and singular purpose. He could be abrupt. In spite of Nehemiah's occasional unorthodox approach to issues, God used this leader's unique personality to accomplish seemingly impossible tasks. It required *cunning* (as when he surveyed the city ruins by night), and *boldness* (as when he locked the gates against merchandisers as the Sabbath began).

We can glean from this study of the book of Nehemiah, as well as the writing from modern-day pastors, that God can take our unique characteristics, refine them and use them for His glory when we offer our lives to Him in glad surrender.

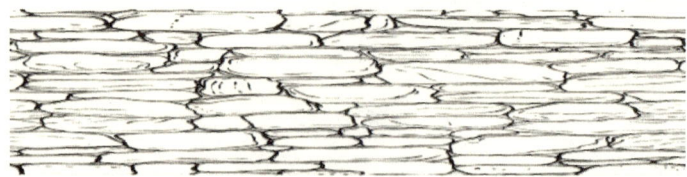

Dear Father in Heaven, I am reminded that You use people of all stripes. I submit to Your leadership in all areas of the ministry that You have given me. I realize that humility is not the same as weakness. Please help me to be bold when needed, and yet retain compassion for the lost. In the name of Your Son, who was our greatest example while on earth, amen.

PARTING THOUGHTS

I discovered the following blog post by Dr. Randall McElwain as I finished the last chapters of this book. God has used Dr. McElwain's teaching ministry around the world. He has served as a pastor and teacher in Kaohsiung, Taiwan. For thirty years, he taught music and Bible at Hobe Sound Bible College. At the time of this writing, he teaches overseas pastors for Shepherds Global Classroom, serves as teaching pastor at Palm Beach Chinese Christian Chapel, and discipleship/teaching pastor at Hobe Sound Bible Church. Dr. McElwain's ministry has been diverse. God uses his unique perspectives to bless many around the world.

"I AM With You Always": Hope for Discouraged Pastors[50]

Printed with permission.

It is Monday morning. Last week you spent hours preparing sermons for Sunday. Yesterday you felt God's help as you shared truth from His Word. Then late last night you received a text: "Pastor, I hope you won't be disappointed, but we have decided to move to XYZ Church. We like your preaching, so don't feel bad. But their worship is more upbeat, and they have a great program for our teens. By the way, thanks for helping our family when I was out of work. And your wife was such a help to our children while Sally was in the hospital last month. Thanks for everything and keep encouraged!"

This morning, you type a resignation letter. Ministry seems hopeless. You study, you pray, you visit, you preach; but the church doesn't grow. You feel that you are fighting a losing battle.

You remember when you were excited about ministry. You were ready to fulfill Jesus's Great Commission in your community. "Go therefore and make disciples of all nations, baptizing them in the name of the Father and of the Son and of the Holy Spirit, teaching them to observe all that I have commanded you." But today, you pastor a small congregation that shares none of your vision for evangelism. You are ready to quit.

Making disciples was never easy, even in the first century. We read Acts and are thrilled by 3,000 converts on the Day of Pentecost. We rejoice when Cornelius is converted; when churches are planted in new cities; and when Paul, the most zealous opponent of the church, is saved. But we must not forget the stoning of Stephen, Peter's imprisonment, and Paul's beatings. Perhaps more relevant to our ministry, we must not forget the days on which there was no persecution, but neither were there any conversions. Even in the first century, there were many days when little happened.

On both difficult days and ordinary days, the apostles lived with this promise: "I am with you always." These words gave hope when the religious leaders beat them, hope when Roman officials arrested them, and hope when they preached but saw no fruit.

The book of Acts begins with Jesus' commission, "You will be my witnesses in Jerusalem and in all Judea and Samaria, and to the end of the earth" (Acts 1:8). Jesus gave his followers an enormous task, but He promised that the Holy Spirit would give the apostles power to accomplish the work.

The book of Acts ends with the Holy Spirit continuing to give the power to accomplish the Great Commission. Even under house arrest, Paul was "proclaiming the kingdom of God and teaching about the Lord Jesus Christ with all boldness and without hindrance" (Acts 28:31). The promise, "I am with you always," was being fulfilled even in Rome.

Today, you may preach and find opposition. You may share the gospel and be mocked. More likely, you may preach to people who politely nod and go away unchanged. You may share the gospel and get a simple, "No, thanks." Regardless of the response, don't lose hope. You are not doing this on your own! The same Jesus who commissioned you to make disciples promised to be with you always. You are not alone.

ACKNOWLEDGMENTS

Sincere thanks to the following pastors and leaders who graciously donated time to write about their experiences. The contributions they penned were exactly what I needed to flesh out principles that are best understood through stories.

Melvin Beecher	Wesley Holden
Norris Belcher	Randall McElwain
Adam Buckler	Garry Spriggs
Haskell Burch	Barry Sweitzer, Jr.
Douglas Evans	William Syfert
Stephen Gibson	Wallace Thornton, Jr.
Roger Hatfield	Alan Walter
Terrie Hay	Brent Woodard
Greg Hobelman	

Pastors seeking further leadership principles can find helpful information in *Ministry Leadership* by Dr. Stephen Gibson of Shepherds Global Classroom. *www.shepherdsglobalclassroom.org*

Heartfelt thanks to my fellow writers in the Word Weavers Page 29 critique group: Debra, Joan, Kathy, Lyneta, and Patricia. Your honest evaluations clarified weak spots in my writing. Your encouragement kept me going when I grew weary.

Lyneta, you are a top-notch editor. You answered my questions so patiently as I struggled to understand tech terms involved in producing this book. If you snickered after answering my questions when I seemed like a first grader in a college physics class, I wouldn't hold it against you. Thanks a million.

ABOUT THE AUTHOR

Roberta Sarver served as a pastor's wife for over thirty years. She observed those behind the pulpit face leadership issues, and as a result, developed heartfelt regard for God's servants standing in the gap for souls.

Beginning university studies as a journalism major and ending with a Bible college degree in English education, she has written interviews for specialty magazines and penned regular newspaper columns. Currently, her blog *Armchair Wit (www.armchairwit.com)* blends inspiration and information, while filling the cultural gap with common sense and occasional humor. Roberta is a contributing author to the book *Radical Abundance,* published in 2022. She is a member of Word Weavers International.

Bibliography

BibleAsk. "Who Were the Ammonites According to the Bible?" Accessed December 8, 2022. https://bibleask.org/who-were-the-ammonites-according-to-the-bible.

Bible Study Tools. "The Samaritans: Hope From the History of a Hated People." Accessed December 6, 2022. https://www.biblestudytools.com/bible-study/topical-studies/the-samaritans-hope-from-the-history-of-a-hated-people.html.

Calvin, John, et al. *1599 Geneva Bible Notes*. Bronson, MI: Online Publishing, 2010. CD-ROM.

British Family Bible. Bronson, MI: Online Publishing, 2010. CD-ROM.

Carry the Light. "Dwight L. Moody." Accessed December 17, 2022. https://www.ctl.today/authors/2020/1/24/dwight-l-moody.

Challies, Tim. "Hymn Stories: Just As I Am." *Challies* (blog). Accessed December 5, 2022. https://www.challies.com/articles/hymn-stories-just-as-i-am/.

Christianity Today. "Fruits of Breaking Wesley's Code." Accessed December 8, 2022. https://www.christianitytoday.com/history/issues/issue-2/fruits-of-breaking-wesleys-code.html.

Clarke, Adam. *Adam Clarke's Commentary*. Bronson, MI: Online Publishing, 2010. CD-ROM.

Cowman, L.B. *Streams in the Desert*. Grand Rapids: Zondervan Publishing House, 1928.

Demaray, C.E. *Beacon Bible Commentary, Volume 2: Joshua through Esther*. Kansas City: Beacon Hill Press, 1965.

Henderson, Daniel. *Old Paths, New Power*. Chicago: Moody Publishers, 2016.

Henry, Matthew. *Matthew Henry Commentary*. Bronson, MI: Online Publishing, 2010. CD-ROM.

Jamieson-Fausset-Brown Bible Commentary. Bronson, MI: Online Publishing, 2010. CD-ROM.

Marshall, Peter and David Manuel. *From Sea to Shining Sea:1737–1837*. Grand Rapids: Fleming H. Revell, 1986.

McElwain, Randall. "I Am With You Always." Accessed December 19, 2022. https://holyjoys.org/hope-discouraged-pastors/.

Metaxas, Eric. *Amazing Grace: William Wilberforce and the Heroic Campaign to End Slavery*. New York: Harper One, 2007.

Meyer, F.B. *Our Daily Homily, Vol II*. Grand Rapids: Zondervan Publishing House, 1951.

Revival Library, The. "Revival in the Hebrides by Duncan Campbell." Accessed December 16, 2022. https://tinyurl.com/ycktvbdm.

Sarver, Roberta. "Celestial Piano Lessons." In *Radical Abundance: More Than All We Can Ask or Imagine,* edited by Teresa Janzen, 24-26. Kalamazoo, MI: Abundance Books, 2022.

Spurgeon, Charles. "Some Go to Church." Accessed December 8, 2022. https://www.azquotes.com/quote/1415988.

---. *Spurgeon's Devotional Commentary*. Bronson, MI: Online Publishing, 2010. CD-ROM.

Strong, James. "Worship." In *Strong's Hebrew Lexicon*. Bronson, MI: Online Publishing, 2010. CD-ROM.

Swindoll, Charles. *Hand Me Another Brick Bible Companion: Timeless Lessons on Leadership*. Nashville: Thomas Nelson, 2006.

Wright, J. Stafford. *Beacon Bible Commentary, Volume 2: Joshua through Esther*. Kansas City: Beacon Hill Press, 1965.

ENDNOTES

Chapter 1

[1] C.E. Demaray, *Beacon Bible Commentary, Volume 2: Joshua through Esther* (Kansas City: Beacon Hill Press, 1965), 632.

[2] Demaray, *Beacon Bible Commentary*, 632.

[3] Tim Challies, "Hymn Stories: Just As I Am," *Challies* (blog), May 12, 2013, https://www.challies.com/articles/hymn-stories-just-as-i-am/.

[4] "Dwight L. Moody," Carry the Light, accessed December 17, 2022, https://www.ctl.today/authors/2020/1/24/dwight-l-moody.

[5] Charles Swindoll, *Hand Me Another Brick Bible Companion: Timeless Lessons on Leadership*, (Nashville: Thomas Nelson, 2006), 21-22

[6] Eric Metaxas, *Amazing Grace: William Wilberforce and the Heroic Campaign to End Slavery*, (New York: Harper One, 2007), 69.

[7] Metaxas, *Amazing Grace*, 76.

[8] Peter Marshall, and David Manuel, *From Sea to Shining Sea: 1737–1837*, (Grand Rapids: Fleming H. Revell, 1986), 62.

Chapter 2

[9] Marshall, *From Sea to Shining Sea*, 68.

[10] Marshall, *From Sea to Shining Sea*, 69.

[11] On this site you can hear Duncan Campbell describing the revival happenings in his delightful Scottish brogue: https://www.youtube.com/watch?v=db9EgMYWTKY.

[12] "Revival in the Hebrides by Duncan Campbell," The Revival Library, accessed December 16, 2022, https://www.revival-library.org/revival_histories/evangelical/twentieth_century/hebrides_revival_2.shtml.

[13] Daniel Henderson, *Old Paths, New Power*, (Chicago: Moody Publishers, 2016), 70.

[14] Swindoll, *Hand Me Another Brick*, 22.

Chapter 3

[15] Demaray, *Beacon Bible Commentary*, 634.

[16] F.B.Meyer, *Our Daily Homily, Vol II.*, (Grand Rapids: Zondervan Publishing House, 1951), 179.

[17] While this may not always be the way to handle a delicate situation of this nature, it was the way God directed in this instance. It is vitally important to handle this issue prayerfully.

[18] "Charles Spurgeon Quotes on Prayer," Bible Apologetics—A Daily Devotional, accessed January 6, 2023, https://bibleapologetics.org/charles-spurgeon-quotes-on-prayer/.

Chapter 4

[19] "The Samaritans: Hope From the History of a Hated People," Bible Study Tools, accessed December 6, 2022, https://www.biblestudytools.com/bible-study/topical-studies/the-samaritans-hope-from-the-history-of-a-hated-people.html.

[20] Demaray, *Beacon Bible Commentary*, 638.

[21] Demaray, *Beacon Bible Commentary*, 638.

[22] "Who Were the Ammonites According to the Bible?" BibleAsk, accessed December 8, 2022, https://bibleask.org/who-were-the-ammonites-according-to-the-bible.

[23] "Who Were the Ammonites According to the Bible?" BibleAsk, accessed December 8, 2022, https://bibleask.org/who-were-the-ammonites-according-to-the-bible.

[24] Demaray, *Beacon Bible Commentary*, 638.

Chapter 5

[25] Roberta Sarver, "Celestial Piano Lessons," *Radical Abundance: More Than All We Can Ask or Imagine*, edited by Teresa Janzen, (Kalamazoo, MI: Abundance Books, 2022), 24–26. Used by permission.

[26] J Stafford Wright, *Beacon Bible Commentary*, 641.

[27] *1599 Geneva Bible Notes*, (Bronson, MI: Online Publishing, 2010), 5.9, CD-ROM.

[28] *Matthew Henry Commentary*, (Bronson, MI: Online Publishing, 2010), 5.9, CD-ROM.

[29] *Jamieson-Fausset-Brown Bible Commentary*, (Bronson, MI: Online Publishing, 2010), 5.9, CD-ROM.

[30] *Adam Clarke's Commentary*, (Bronson, MI: Online Publishing, 2010), 5.9, CD-ROM.

Chapter 6

[31] L.B. Cowman, *Streams in the Desert*, (Grand Rapids: Zondervan Publishing House, 1928), Sept. 22nd entry by C.H. Spurgeon.

Chapter 8

[32] To find out more, visit https://ministeringtoministers.org/, call 404-687-4577, or email mtm@ctsnet.edu.

[33] "Fruits of Breaking Wesley's Code," *Christianity Today*, accessed December 8, 2022, https://www.christianitytoday.com/history/issues/issue-2/fruits-of-breaking-wesleys-code.html.

Chapter 9

[34] *Adam Clarke's Commentary*, (Bronson, MI: Online Publishing, 2010), 5.9, CD-ROM.

[35] *Matthew Henry Commentary*," (Bronson, MI: Online Publishing, 2010), 5.9, CD-ROM.

[36] *Spurgeon's Devotional Commentary*," (Bronson, MI: Online Publishing, 2010), 5.9, CD-ROM.

Chapter 10

[37] *Spurgeon's Devotional Commentary*," (Bronson, MI: Online Publishing, 2010), 5.9, CD-ROM.

[38] Demaray, *Beacon Bible Commentary*, 652.

[39] *Beacon Bible Commentary*, 652.

[40] *Beacon Bible Commentary*, 652–653.

[41] *Adam Clarke's Commentary*, (Bronson, MI: Online Publishing, 2010), 5.9, CD-ROM.

Chapter 11

[42] *Strong's Hebrew Lexicon*, (1979), "worship."

[43] Charles Spurgeon, "Some Go to Church," *AZ Quotes,* accessed December 8, 2022, https://www.azquotes.com/quote/1415988.

[44] *Beacon Bible Commentary*, 656.

Chapter 12

[45] *Beacon Bible Commentary*, 664.

[46] *Beacon Bible Commentary*, 663.

[47] *Adam Clarke's Commentary*," (Bronson, MI: Online Publishing, 2010), 5.9, CD-ROM.

[48] *British Family Bible*," (Bronson, MI: Online Publishing, 2010), 5.9, CD-ROM.

[49] *Spurgeon's Devotional Commentary*, (Bronson, MI: Online Publishing, 2010), 5.9, CD-ROM.

Parting Thoughts

[50] Randall McElwain, "I Am With You Always," accessed December 19, 2022, https://holyjoys.org/hope-discouraged-pastors/.